Integrating GIS and the
Global Positioning System

Karen Steede–Terry

ESRI PRESS

Published by
Environmental Systems Research Institute, Inc.
380 New York Street
Redlands, California 92373-8100

Environmental Systems Research Institute, Inc.

Integrating GIS and the Global Positioning System
ISBN 1-879102-81-1

Contents

The space station is orbiting the earth at an altitude of about 200 miles. It's an exciting piece of space technology, and gets a lot of press. Another 12,400 miles beyond it, however, a constellation of satellites—twenty-four of them, and a few spares—is having a less spectacular but quite possibly more profound impact on the way we manage and govern our affairs here on earth, the way we navigate and map, track and investigate, document our lives and inform ourselves.

The Global Positioning System, with its ability to generate accurate positional data, is uniquely suited to integration with GIS. Whether the object of our concern is moving or not, whether our concern is for a certain place at a certain time, a series of places over time, or a place with no regard to time, GPS can measure it, locate it, track it—all that's missing is a context for that data.

As the Internet rapidly changes our notions of what kinds of information are available—and to whom, at what price—the usefulness of a GIS as a means of organizing, analyzing, and exploring data becomes quite striking.

It is in fact a necessity: our world is being digitized, and while gaining access to that digital data is now relatively easy, making sense of it, using it, is not—without the right tools. If we as a society are to share this information efficiently, effectively, democratically, our basic need becomes one of education: what skills must we learn, and how are other people and organizations applying those skills? It is to that end that this book presents the variety of experiences and stories it does.

Most of the people featured in these case studies are pioneers in their field. From mapping energy pipelines to broadcasting yacht races on the Internet, from tracking disease-carrying sand flies to monitoring lime distribution in cornfields, they have built, and continue to build, the foundations of a truly "societal GIS"—an integration of two powerful technologies that can only help us live more peaceful and productive lives in the coming century.

Jack Dangermond
President, ESRI

Acknowledgments

This book is the culmination of the experience and knowledge of many people. I wish to thank all of the contributors, whose efforts made the final manuscript possible.

First and foremost, I am very grateful to all of the interview subjects. This book would not be possible without their cooperation, knowledge, insights, and use of GIS and GPS technology. You'll find those individuals acknowledged by name at the end of each case study.

I interviewed several people who have not been featured in the case studies; their contributions were nevertheless crucially important to the integrity of the book. It would not have been possible to complete it without the sage advice of Gretchen Hartley, Trimble Navigation, Ltd., and Peter Price, an independent GIS, GPS, and remote sensing consultant in Houston, Texas. You will find their knowledge sprinkled throughout the book.

Marj Dougherty of ESRI gave me many story ideas and contact information. Michele Mason provided me with invaluable graphics support, in addition to the many talented people at ESRI. Thanks in particular to Jennifer Galloway, who did the page layout and all production and image editing. Tammy Johnson designed the cover. There are also many people who provided valuable information and references. Although not specifically mentioned by name, thanks are due all of them.

I also wish to thank Gary Amdahl of ESRI for writing chapter 12 on the topic of Web-based real-time maps, but most of all for his professionalism and patience during the editing process.

I am especially grateful to Christian Harder and Jack Dangermond at ESRI, who gave me the opportunity to put my knowledge and thoughts into this published account.

Finally, words cannot express the appreciation and gratitude I have for the support of my husband, David Terry. As a user of GIS and GPS himself, he not only assisted me with many of the ideas, information, and graphics found throughout the book, but he also put up with a lot of long hours and late nights!

•••••• An introduction to the Global Positioning System

Cops chasing robbers in Maine . . . biologists tracking parasites carrying a fatal, infectious disease in Texas . . . retirees planning to build a dock on their new lakeshore property in Arkansas . . . a lone sailor in the middle of the Atlantic, his keel fouled with flotsam . . . a farmer high atop his combine in Minnesota . . . an old elephant on her way to the mythical graveyard somewhere in the Great Rift Valley of Kenya—Quick, what do all these situations have in common? Satellites and radio receivers packed with astonishingly flexible software: the Global Positioning System (GPS).

Use of the Global Positioning System—a way of accurately determining positions on the surface of the earth—has grown exponentially since it became feasible for commercial use in the early 1990s. Designed and developed originally for military use only, GPS is now used in mapping, navigation, surveying, agriculture, construction, vehicle tracking and recovery, archaeology, biology—the list goes on and on. In fact, GPS has become so widely used that it has now even found its way into a wide range of consumer products, from cell phones and automobiles to handheld "personal" receivers that have tumbled in cost from around $2,000 (the 1990 figure) to under $100. GPS chips are now being heavily used in computer networks, and popping up as well in such unlikely places as ATMs and the entire range of mobile communications equipment.

The worldwide annual market this year will be something like $11 billion, and its effects will be felt virtually everywhere. But perhaps nowhere has the impact of GPS been as great, or the benefits as real, as for users of geographic information systems (GIS). Organizations that maintain spatial databases—local governments, oil and gas companies, forest product companies, among many others—can now easily and accurately inventory the location of their assets in the field and add these locations to their GIS databases. Assets that can be measured and inventoried with GPS include stationary things like manholes, sewer

lines, pipelines, and trees; and moving things, like motor vehicles, animals, and ships. In fact, the capability of GPS to track moving things over time has opened a whole new area of GIS, known as temporal–spatial analysis.

A GIS is a "graphic database," or an "intelligent map," that stores and displays the points, lines (series of points), and areas (connected lines) of GPS data as features (items) and attributes (records, names, descriptions). GIS is a tool that can capture data (through digitizing and other methods), store it, analyze it, retrieve it, and make maps from it. Cities

grow, new subdivisions are built, and neighborhood demographics change. Soils are depleted, stands of timber cut down. Endangered species flee the country. In short, GIS data is dynamic, and GPS is a phenomenally effective way to track those changes.

Part one of this book walks you through the fundamentals of the system, and discusses some of the issues that will come up as you attempt to integrate GPS data into your GIS. Part two is a collection of case studies that examine some of the ways people have been using GPS and GIS technology together.

What exactly is the GPS?

The Global Positioning System is a constellation of twenty-seven NAVSTAR satellites orbiting the earth at a height of
12,600 miles; five monitoring stations (in
Hawaii, Ascension Island, Diego Garcia,
Kwajalein, and exotic Colorado Springs);
and individual receivers. By reading the
radio signal broadcast from as few as
three of these satellites simultaneously
(a process known as trilateration), a
receiver on earth can pinpoint its exact
location on the ground. This location is
expressed in latitude and longitude
coordinates.

Fortunately for people who wish to use
GPS to fix locations, they need not even
think about the satellites or the monitoring stations. Just like radio or broadcast
television signals, GPS signals are available to anyone who has the proper equipment and knowledge. The twenty-four
active satellites (there are currently three
spares up there, too) have been deployed
in six evenly distributed orbits, at speeds
that have each satellite passing over a
monitoring station once every twelve
hours. That means there are always more
than four visible in the sky everywhere
on the planet. The satellites continuously
transmit signals on two L-band frequencies, and the monitoring stations send
correctional data to keep the satellites
trim and exactly where they're supposed
to be.

*The satellites are deployed in a pattern
that has each one passing over a
monitoring station every twelve
hours, with at least four visible in
the sky at all times.*

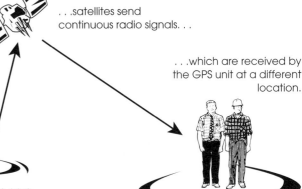

*The satellites transmit
a continuous radio
signal on the L-band,
in pseudorandom
code, to ground
receivers, and receive
correctional data from
monitoring stations.*

. . .satellites send
continuous radio signals. . .

. . .which are received by
the GPS unit at a different
location.

A monitoring station on a
remote island sends correctional
data to satellites. . .

Who built it and why?

Many of us take for granted the ability to pinpoint our precise whereabouts on the great global grid, those imaginary lines of latitude and longitude (add a third measurement, elevation, and what you've got is called a graticule). It's hard to imagine a time when figuring locations wasn't nearly so easy. Early sailors navigated as best they could by using landmarks and positions of the sun and the stars. Shipwrecks due to faulty navigation were commonplace. Explorers of the New World confined their travel as much as possible to known lines of latitude because they had no way of determining longitude—and were therefore easy prey for pirates lounging in those same lanes. Only with the development of accurate seaworthy chronometers by the British in the late 18th century did navigators finally have a way of determining a more or less exact location on earth—an advancement so significant that it led to Great Britain's emergence as a world power.

The thorniest scientific problem of the 18th century was solved by a genius clockmaker named John Harrison. His marine chronometers allowed ocean navigators to know exactly what time it was in two places at once, and thus have the key to unlocking the mystery of longitude. From left to right: four successive versions of Harrison's chronometers, from the early large and elaborate models to the pocket watch.

Images courtesy National Maritime Museum

One of the first electronic navigation tools was a radio-based system called LORAN. It's still in use today (LORAN-C, along with DECCA, a European counterpart), guiding ships in coastal and intracontinental waters via triangulation from stationary ground-based radio transmitters. Recent advances in coverage (filling the midcontinent gap) have made the service useful to terrestrial navigators as well. The system's major drawback remains its lack of fine-tunability: measurements are accurate only to within approximately 300 meters.

With the dawn of the space age and orbiting satellites came the opportunity to create a much more accurate navigation system that could be used from anywhere on earth. The military applications were obvious, but the cost enormous, so it's not surprising that the original Global Positioning System was conceived, designed, and ultimately deployed by the U.S. Department of Defense (DoD).

Despite the high cost, the U.S. Congress (partly in response to severe communication and logistical problems suffered by U.S. forces in the Vietnam conflict) voted in 1976 to approve and fund the development of GPS technology, first and foremost as a matter of national defense. Thankfully, however, they also anticipated how valuable the technology could be for business and the general public, and thus allowed for the eventual declassification of the technology for commercial use.

The Gulf War in 1990 gave the U.S. military its first opportunity to really test the system—and it was hugely successful in keeping troops organized on the ground. Considering, then, that GPS has only been working as a completely operational system for about a decade, it's truly remarkable how rapidly and extensively the technology has been applied.

LORAN was the first electronic navigation tool and the forerunner of the global positioning system.

GPS was so successful in the Gulf War that the Pentagon purchased an additional nine thousand handheld units halfway through the operation.

The GPS market

Since 1984, when the first commercial GPS receiver was put on the market, sales of GPS technology have increased sharply. By 1991, worldwide sales revenue of receivers was about $300 million; by 1995 it was approximately $700 million, and by 1997, almost $2 billion. The worldwide market for GPS products and services is predicted to reach at least $14 billion by the year 2005, and possibly go as high as $31 billion. Gains are being seen in all markets, including in-vehicle navigation, communications equipment, vehicle/freight tracking, agriculture, aviation, marine systems, and surveying and mapping equipment.

Steadily decreasing cost of hardware and steadily increasing use of embedded software are the two major factors making commercial use easier and more broadly applicable. A third factor is a decision recently made (days before this book went to press) by the Clinton administration to discontinue the Department of Defense's intentional garbling of the GPS signal. Selective Availability, or S/A, has been used by the DoD since the system's earliest days as a way of limiting its effectiveness by persons or countries bent on sabotage. By introducing a random timing error to the satellite signal, the accuracy of readings had been off by as much as 100 meters.

Partly as a consequence of advances in GPS technology—particularly the techniques of differential correction (DGPS) on one hand, and more effective GPS

jamming devices on the other—and partly in response to competitive pressures from the European Union's Galileo positioning system, discontinuation of S/A had been in the works for some time. The Clinton administration announced in 1996 that S/A would be "reevaluated" in 2000, but some estimates had the shutoff date as late as 2006. Its termination this year was something of a surprise, but certainly a pleasant one for the industry.

A budget initiative was also announced by the office of the vice president in early 1999, calling for two more civilian signals to be added to the satellite broadcast by no later than 2005, a "safety of life" emergency services signal, and a corrective signal that will reduce distortions caused by the broadcast's passage through the atmosphere.

The steadily decreasing size of GPS receivers is making field use as easy as carrying a cell phone, and contributing as well to the explosive growth and expansion of the market.

Photo courtesy Trimble Navigation, Ltd.

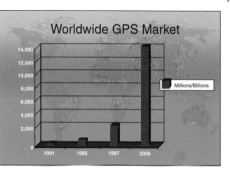

Worldwide GPS Market

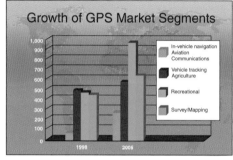

Growth of GPS Market Segments

How the system works

For all the technical complexity of satellites and space launches, GPS works according to a fairly simple principle: it uses the length of time it takes a signal to travel from a satellite to a receiver on the ground to calculate that satellite's distance from the receiver. GPS satellites transmit continuous streams of coded radio signals that indicate their position in space and the exact time that signals are being sent. Theoretically, with a perfect clock, signals from three satellites would be enough information for a receiver to compute its position and express it as a coordinate of latitude and longitude. But because the perfect clock doesn't quite exist—and a discrepancy between satellite and receiver timing of just 1/100th of a second could make for a misreading of 1,860 miles—a fourth satellite and measurement is necessary. And with that fourth signal, GPS receivers can fix an elevation.

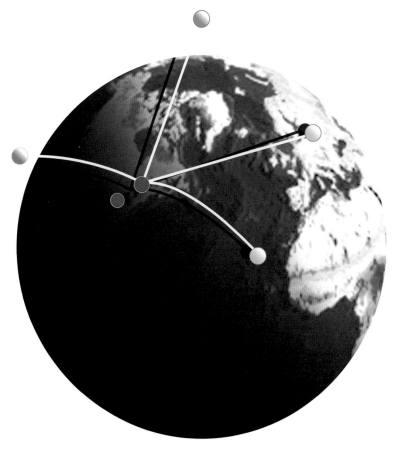

A timing error of 1/100th of a second would place you in the Hudson Bay when you thought you were in New York City.

Measuring distance by measuring time

How can a GPS receiver really know exactly how far it is from a satellite? The answer is that it measures time to calculate the distance using that old grade-school standby equation, *distance = time × velocity*. The velocity in the equation is a constant (relatively speaking—more on this later) because the signal travels at the speed of light. So in order to complete the equation, the receiver needs to know only how long it took for the signal to travel from the satellite to the GPS receiver on the ground. Because the time measurement needed is so short (nanoseconds), both the receiver and the satellite have to keep extremely accurate time in order for a true position to be calculated. To accomplish this, each GPS satellite is equipped with an atomic clock (so-called not because it's atomic-powered, but because

it records the metronome-like bouncing of a particular atom), and GPS receivers with quartz clocks. If there is a time discrepancy between the satellite and the receiver, the receiver's clock is automatically adjusted by the satellites. Once the radio signals have been received from the satellite, the GPS receiver has only to note the difference between the time the signal left the satellite and the time the receiver got it.

Without getting too technical, the method by which that difference is noted goes something like this: the signal the satellites are transmitting is an extremely complicated alternation of bits, ones and zeros in a pattern that repeats every 1,023 bits. It's so complicated that the pattern looks random, like background noise, and thus is called the "pseudorandom

code." There's not a whole lot of information in this signal—that's why the satellites and receivers both don't have to be so high-powered their expense becomes prohibitive. It's simply—and very ingeniously—a timing signal. The GPS receiver notes that one particular peak or trough of a bit is this many millionths of a second off when it compares its section of code to the satellite's, and there it is: the time, the velocity, the distance.

The atom in an atomic clock oscillates at a rate of about 9.2 billion times per second.

Time difference between same part of code

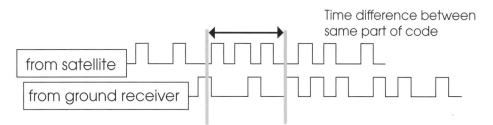

Why a code?

The pseudorandom code has other functions: because its complicated variations can so easily be distinguished (with the proper receiver, of course), each satellite can transmit its own unique code and thus have an identity uniquely its own. The code also helps the system resist jamming and interference: the pseudorandom code carried on a GPS signal can only be recognized by a GPS receiver. Finally, the code makes it possible for the satellites to transmit on only two frequencies, L1 and L2, without confusion.

What the reading tells us

You are in the field preparing to record some positions. You turn the receiver on, it begins to receive signals from a satellite, and it provides a latitude/longitude coordinate almost instantly. It's also scanning the skies for the next satellite. The first measurement tells you only that you are somewhere on the earth's surface (news that may or may not be helpful to you). The second measurement, from a second satellite, dramatically narrows the possibilities. The third satellite gives the receiver enough information to calculate its location as one of two points. Often, one of these points can be quickly discarded as not possible—it has you dangling in midair, for instance. Most of the time, however, because of the tiny but important errors inherent in the system, a fourth measurement is necessary. The fourth satellite allows the receiver to eliminate one of the two points, resulting in a location you can log in three dimensions—accurate, depending on equipment and circumstances, from 10 to 15 meters (now that S/A is off) down to mere centimeters.

Two measurements will place us somewhere inside this circle

The first reading puts you somewhere on the globe. The second narrows the possibilities to the circle where the two globes intersect. The third places you at one of the two points (one of which can usually be disregarded).

Three measurements will place us at one of two points

GPS accuracy

It is important to recognize that while a GPS receiver returns an exact coordinate, there is some inescapable uncertainty that goes along with every measurement. As ingenious as the system is, there are several sources of error that can reduce the accuracy of a reading. Some of these are random in nature, and beyond our control; others are systematic and therefore open to suggestion. What this means for the user is that out-of-the-box accuracy for GPS receivers can range from 10 to 15 meters. The good news is that there are methods of correction, known collectively as "differential GPS," that can increase the level of accuracy down, in some cases, to just a few inches.

Signal degradation: What it is and why it is

GPS readings are less than perfectly accurate because the signals become degraded in the fraction of a second it takes them to travel from satellite to receiver. With S/A turned off (keep in mind the DoD retains the power to turn it back on should need arise), the accuracy of GPS positions increases from 100 meters to about 15, and most users will also notice more accurate z values (elevation data). There are several other factors, however, contributing significant amounts of distortion as well. The key to overcoming signal degradation is to understand what causes it.

The
Speed of Light
is Relative, too . . .

Several factors affect the accuracy of the GPS signal; the gravitational pulls of the sun and the moon, a not-quite-constant speed of light, and receiver noise can throw a location off by as much as 10 meters.

Unintentional degradation

Because GPS satellites orbit the planet at an altitude of more than 12,600 miles (making their orbits less subject to interference and thereby more predictable), their signals must pass through all the layers of the earth's atmosphere before reaching a GPS receiver on the ground. As they pass through layers like the troposphere (where our weather occurs) and the ionosphere (a band of densely packed ions and free electrons, between 80 and 120 miles up), the signals are delayed. Yes: Einstein's infamously constant speed of light is actually slowed down by that thick band of charged particles, and by water vapor, too. This delay obviously affects the $d=vt$ equation, and consequently the accuracy of the GPS receiver's calculation of position.

Another category of error is called "ephemeris." These are minor disturbances of satellite orbit caused by the sun and the moon: gravitational pulls and the pressure of solar radiation. Those five monitoring stations run by the DoD regularly transmit correctional data to the satellites as they pass overhead, each one of them, twice a day.

A third source of error can be traced back to the nearly perfect atomic clocks aboard the satellites. Sometimes they're wrong! The deviations are extremely small, and the monitoring stations make timing as well as orbit adjustments, but remember: 1/100th of a second can put you on another continent!

Error number four: the receiver itself. Receiver accuracy varies greatly, and depends on what the unit is designed to do, the kind of GPS chip it's got, whether or not it can reject errors, and, of course, cost. Many of the more sophisticated receivers on the market today have built-in software that can automatically correct all sorts of errors—atmospheric, for instance, by averaging delays—but that doesn't prevent them from making mistakes on their own. Computational in nature, for the most part, stemming from faulty clocks or internal noise, the mistakes are either very big and easily detectable, or very small, making for decreases of accuracy in the range of a few feet.

The final kind of error is the same sort of disturbed picture you see on your TV set when "ghost" or multiple shadow images appear. This phenomenon is called "multipath" and occurs when the signal bounces around off larger reflective surfaces or objects near your receiver. The receiver hears several signals and doesn't know which one to choose. Again, the better receivers today can correct multipath errors.

A dedicated system

Another, less annoying, safeguard built into GPS by the DoD is that GPS satellites are what is called a dedicated system: the satellites can't be used for any other purpose. This is so operations won't be disrupted during times of crisis, and the military can move them to wherever they need them. An example of this was in the 1991 Gulf War, when the majority of the GPS satellites were repositioned over the Persian Gulf. Right now, most of the satellites in the constellation are able to communicate only with the monitoring stations, making repositioning a "first come, first served" operation, laborious and time-consuming. The next generation of satellites, however, will be able to talk to each other. A single message from a monitoring station will be passed around to all the satellites in the constellation, dramatically speeding up the repositioning process in times of national crisis.

Cooking raw GPS data in the GIS kitchen

The signals fall from the sky at the speed of light, the receiver instantly translates them into latitude and longitude coordinates—Now what? What you've got in hand—literally—is raw geographic information. But the point "95 degrees N, 30 degrees W" is not especially meaningful, in and of itself, to most people. It would be like a TV weathercaster reporting high and low temperatures across the country without a map underlying them. The next step is to cook that data in a GIS.

The new generation of global positioning satellites will be able to talk to each other, one receiving information from a monitoring station and passing it on to the next. Boeing, the manufacturer, hopes for launches sometime in 2001.

Chapter 2

●●●●●● Differential GPS

Errors revisited

All those types of error we introduced in the last chapter—the not-quite-constant speed of light, faulty clocks, ephemeris variations, receiver fuzziness, multipath "ghosting"—contribute bulk to the imaginary line we draw from the satellites to our position. That is, the line is not nice and thin, but thick with uncertainty. The point we get is more like a box. We are somewhere within that box.

Buyer beware

The more sophisticated receivers can correct atmospheric and multipath errors, and can therefore be accurate—when the GPS data is differentially corrected—anywhere from 5-meter to sub-meter range. Some manufacturers use various stratagems that make it seem like their units counter these effects, but in fact they do not.

One trick, known as map-matching, snaps the GPS position on-screen to the nearest road or hiking trail, making the cursor seem like it's exactly on that road. One amused user tells of an in-vehicle navigation system that continued to track the car's position even after it had entered a parking garage. The position, obviously, was interpolated, as GPS is a line-of-sight technology. Satellite signals cannot penetrate buildings.

Many manufacturers have added a feature to their GPS units that will do "instant averaging" in the field. This feature collects more than one position at each waypoint and averages them. The idea is that the average of many positions is likely to be better than any single position. Many GPS users assume that with S/A now off, they can average positions instead of differentially correcting them. This is not true. It sounds like a great way around the problem, but several inaccurate readings do not necessarily make one accurate reading.

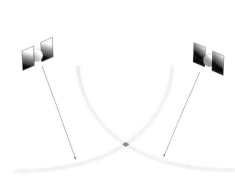

When the satellites are at a wide angle, the positioning "box" is small.

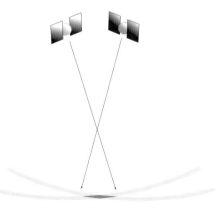

As the satellites get closer to each other, the positioning box gets larger and less accurate.

Differential correction

Differential GPS (or DGPS) is the revolution within the revolution. And of course the principle driving it is very simple: use two receivers. The downside, obviously, is a doubling of cost. But if the application you're considering calls for more stringent standards of accuracy, the investment is relatively small and certainly cost-effective. It brings accuracy into the few-meter range.

Place one receiver at a known location—an accurately surveyed point. This is the base station. The other receiver, the rover, you carry around with you, logging latitude/longitude coordinates. The base station receiver compares where the satellite signals say it is with where it knows it is. The difference is the amount of error. The satellites are so far away that if the two receivers are close to each other—say within 300 miles—they will be subject to the same amount of error, having traveled through more or less the same corridor of atmosphere.

Generally, if the rover is within a hundred miles of a base station, the resulting positions will be accurate to within the specifications of the receiver. The farther away you are, the less accurate the positions will be. If the rover is 100 to 200 miles from the base, accuracy will be approximately two times worse than receiver

specs; if the rover is 200 to 300 miles away, accuracy will be two-and-a-half to three times poorer than spec. Recent advances in technology have made it possible to process over distances greater than 300 miles, but decreased accuracy is still a factor.

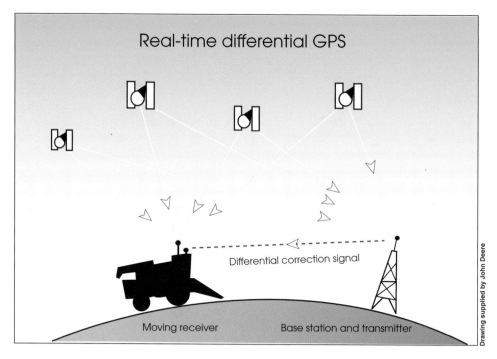

Real-time differential GPS

Differential correction signal

Moving receiver   Base station and transmitter

Drawing supplied by John Deere

Real-time versus postprocessing

First, a word of caution: it's not a good idea to rely on uncorrected GPS data, even with S/A turned off. S/A's absence benefits mainly people using GPS for real-time navigation or autonomous positioning (Automatic Vehicle Location, for example), as well as recreational users: hikers, campers, anglers. Even though data collected without interference from S/A may be off by only 10 to 15 meters, the data can still be shifted from its actual position, and lines or polygons can appear spiky instead of straight. Also, keep in mind that the DoD can scramble the GPS signal anytime it needs to. If you want the accuracy your receiver is built to deliver, you have to differentially correct your data.

You can apply differential corrections in the field when the data is collected, in real time, or after the data has already been collected, using a technique called "postprocessing." Real-time correction is principally for applications like navigation: you're moving, and want to know where you are as you move. Postprocessing is for applications in which you need to know where something is so you can do something with that knowledge, like make a map or survey a new road.

Real-time processing is generally less accurate than postprocessing. Say that you record a location as you drive along. The location is recorded and corrected in seconds or less. If you stand at a location, you can record positions for as long as you like. Back in the office, the GPS software will differentially correct each individual position and then average the positions to obtain the final location. The longer you stood there recording positions, the more positions are available to average when the data is postprocessed, and the more accurate the final position.

Real-time corrections are broadcast during data collection to a GPS receiver in the field from a base station or other source via a radio hookup. The only problem is the time the base station takes to transmit its data—the receiver's latency period. As circumstances in the field are always changing, corrections must always be changing, too, and some receiver-radio links transmit at a baud rate that makes for ten-second delays: maybe a crucial delay, maybe not, but five seconds is generally thought to be the better interval.

Postprocessing is typically done back in the office using special software to compare the data in a rover file to the data received from a base station, and to correct the data in the rover file. To apply postprocessed corrections, your receiver must be capable of storing a file containing not just positions but also the information needed to perform the corrections (offset, distance, rover settings, date, time, and so forth), and have an accompanying software program that can perform the corrections after the data has been collected.

If you purchase a second unit to use as a base, and you intend to postprocess the data, make sure the unit has enough memory and file storage space to accommodate at least six to eight hours of logging. If you plan to use the unit for a real-time broadcast, you must have a wireless radio link. If you are working close to an available base station (within 2 or 3 miles), setting up a radio link between the base and the receiver can be relatively easy; over longer distances, a license from the Federal Communications Commission (FCC) may be necessary.

Differential correction can improve the accuracy of your positions anywhere from 5 meters to under 1 meter, depending on the type of GPS receiver, but please note that these are horizontal accuracies. Horizontal accuracy is one to three times better than vertical accuracy. This is because there are no satellites that we can access below the visible horizon (the earth itself blocks them), so a GPS receiver is limited in its ability to receive accurate height measurements.

Sources of DGPS, for free and for hire

The U.S. Coast Guard has placed several beacons in coastal areas of the United States, as well as along the Mississippi River. These beacons broadcast real-time differential correction for GPS receivers, and were used originally to help ships correct S/A interference and navigate shallow harbors, narrow channels, and busy shipping lanes.

A beacon transmits the corrections for a GPS signal at a given moment, on a very low frequency, in the 200- to 300-MHz range. The beacon signal itself is available free of charge; however, since the GPS signal transmits in the 1,500-MHz frequency range, most GPS receivers require a separate antenna to pick up the beacon's signal. Only a few GPS receivers have integrated antennas to communicate directly with a beacon. But most GPS manufacturers, as well as some third-party manufacturers, make and sell beacon receivers that can be attached to GPS units.

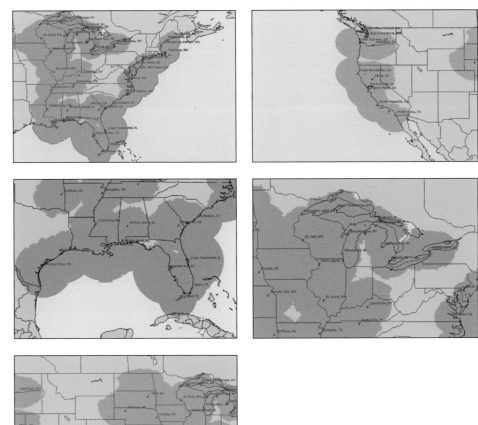

Correctional data is free—if you are close enough to a beacon.

According to the Coast Guard, a beacon has an official range of 150 miles. However, that range varies based on the topography of the area that you are working in. Over the ocean and in extremely flat areas, the beacon's range may be much farther than 150 miles—no absolute distance has been determined. By contrast, if there are hills between you and the beacon, chances are the signal could be intermittent at best. Distance and reception are important, as the farther away you are from the beacon, the less accurate your resulting position will be.

Most GPS users who live in coastal areas choose the U.S. Coast Guard beacons as their method of differential correction—the only cost involved is the receiver required to capture the beacon transmission. If you don't have access to a beacon, you can acquire differential correction from a third party. There are companies selling real-time correction as a service to GPS users. Some piggyback corrections on existing radio frequencies by surveying in the radio broadcast tower as a known coordinate. Others use geosynchronous satellites (GPS satellites are sun-synchronous) to transmit differential correction signals. Users must purchase equipment to receive the real-time signal, or purchase a GPS unit with an integrated antenna capable of receiving both the GPS and differential signals, as well as pay an annual subscription fee for the service. A list of providers of real-time differential correction services can be found at http://gauss.gge.unb.ca/manufact.htm.

In some areas, no real-time differential correction service is available at all. If that's the case, you'll need to postprocess your readings. Most GPS users who live inland choose this method. There is a good chance that there will be a base station within 300 miles of your data collection area. Universities, government agencies, and private companies who are already operating base stations frequently post data on the Internet. In years past, base files had to be downloaded to a floppy disk and mailed to requestors. The Internet has immensely speeded up this process. Once a file is downloaded, postprocessing is usually a simple matter of pressing another button in the GPS software.

Some words of caution if you are going to use someone else's base station. Before using data from a base station that is not your own, you will want to check the accuracy of the base station coordinates.

Has the base station been surveyed in? One would think the obvious answer would be "yes," but you might be surprised how many times this is not the case. One user who wished to remain anonymous tells a story about the city he worked for completely paving over or moving survey markers, and then putting them back over newly poured concrete at random. The lesson here is to be careful about trusting somebody else's "surveyed" coordinates.

You will also need to know if the base station has a clear view of the sky, and how often it logs positions. Does it operate twenty-four hours a day, or only from nine to five? If you need to work on the weekends, make sure the base station data is available first. If the base station isn't operating, and you don't have a base file to work with, you won't be able to postprocess.

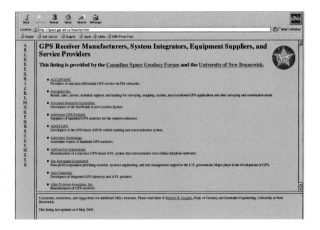

Real-time radio signals can only travel over limited distances. Only recently has access to real-time wide-area differential correction become available in the United States. However, as GPS works by line-of-sight, both radio and satellite signals can be blocked by objects such as buildings or trees. Postprocessing can be performed anywhere, as live communication between the base and the rover is not necessary.

Before you buy a GPS unit, find out how available real-time differential correction will be. Real-time service varies greatly. An organization working overseas purchased a GPS unit that fit its budget, but could only perform real-time correction in the field using a differential beacon signal from the U.S. Coast Guard. Unfortunately, there are only a few beacons available internationally, and none where they were working. Most international users of GPS technology postprocess their data, but this unit was not capable of postprocessing with S/A in effect. The GPS receiver this organization had bought was essentially useless once they took it overseas. (Now that S/A is off, they are luckily back in business.)

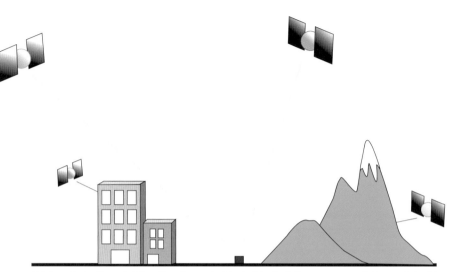

GPS works by line of sight. Signals can be blocked by buildings, trees, and the earth itself.

Chapter 3

Three stages of a GPS project: Planning, implementation, evaluation

One: Planning, or first things first

It's easy to spend money

Before you buy your GPS equipment, plan your project. That's easy to say. It's also easy to spend a lot of money on a system that proves less than ideal in actual use. What kind of field conditions—weather and terrain—will prevail? How sturdy must the unit be? Will you be driving most of the time? Bicycling? Walking? Do you need a digital background map or aerial photo on display while you're taking readings? If you're collecting feature and attribute data that will be entered into a GIS database, you'll need a unit that can store a full data dictionary (a database that allows a user to enter information about the data being collected).

There are three basic types of GPS unit: handheld models, higher-end backpack rigs, and PC-MCIA cards that run with software on laptop or palmtop computers.

Balance cost and accuracy; it's just as possible to spend too little money—on equipment that gathers dust in a storage locker—as it is to spend too much. Can you live with differentially corrected readings in the 1- to 5-meter range? If so, a substantially less expensive midlevel handheld model might be more appropriate—and easier to get approval for—than a more richly featured backpack model. If submeter accuracy is paramount, then you have little choice: you'll have to make that initial investment. If your project will keep you behind the wheel most of the time, the laptop is hard to beat.

Photo courtesy Trimble Navigation, Ltd., and Topcon

Photo courtesy Mike Hobbs and Off-Road.com

With an explosion of innovation, the GPS hardware industry is responsible for making the technology practical and affordable.

Pilot project and field reconnaissance

Review the existing operations and needs of your organization, and decide how and where your GPS project is going to fit in. Work out the parameters of your project on a small scale—i.e., develop a pilot project—and test it by performing a field reconnaissance: actually going into the field with a notebook. This step will help you and your team more clearly understand the scope of the project, its goals, and the means by which these goals will most efficiently and effectively be realized. Potential problems can be spotted before they become actual. You can plan start and stop points and times, logging intervals, estimate how much work you can get done before your batteries fade, and so on. Field reconnaissance also allows you to identify objects that will be defined as features and attributes in your data dictionary.

Educate the decision makers

Now that you've done your homework, gotten over that sense of being a little kid in a candy shop, and tested your thinking with a field trip, you'll need to educate the decision makers. Most managers will approve a GPS project if you can justify the initial cost with assurances of savings of time or money in the long run. The questions you'll have to answer (and perhaps ask first) are:

How important is locational accuracy to the relevancy and effective use of the data you acquire in the field?

How efficient and productive is your current field work? Are you getting the data you want in time for it to be useful? What's the "life cycle" of your data— how long is it good and what makes it go bad? How hard is it to update your data or revise your needs?

How efficient and productive is your office work? How much time are you spending transferring field data to your database and end-user applications? How much lag time is there between raw data and usable information? Is the project cost-effective?

Solicit not only approval of your project from upper management, but ongoing support for it. In the absence of such support, the well of initial enthusiasm will run dry if management sees no obvious, striking, short-term benefit of using the GPS equipment. This isn't a call for bells and whistles, but an understanding that the real benefits of GPS may not be readily apparent. One GPS consultant puts it this way: "In most cases, selling the concept of GPS data acquisition to clients or management has not been a problem. The problems are in explaining the requirements and limitations of the technology. Managers have seen the inexpensive units at sporting goods stores, and need to be educated on the limitations of these systems. Acquisition limitations, logistical problems, and postprocessing also need to be understood."

Ongoing support means ongoing education.

Next time you see someone on the street with an antenna sticking out of his backpack, you can figure he pretty much knows exactly where he is.

The work-flow chart

The next task is to chart work flow: how and when things will be done, and who will do them. Inventory the tasks involved. This is especially important in a GPS project, as there are a number of equally important tasks surrounding the central activity—field data collection—including creating a data dictionary and integrating it with your GIS database, checking satellite availability, configuring the receivers, downloading data, exporting it to the GIS, revising procedures based on actual field conditions and experience, and maintaining equipment. You can group these tasks—and therefore chart them—in two ways: before, during, and after data collection; and office, field, or either. Break these tasks down: how will each be performed, and in what order?

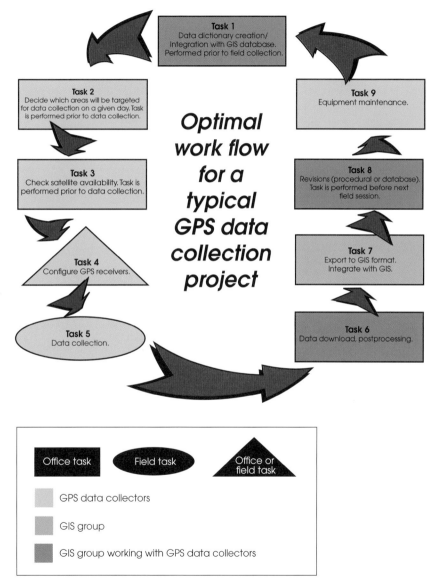

From what to who

Now that you know "what," the question is "who?" How many people will you have to work with? Will there be one group doing everything? A typical scenario has one group in the field and another in the office. More than likely, the GIS group will also want to be involved. Whatever the situation, the point is that tasks need to be clearly delineated and understood ahead of time by the people who will be performing them. Make sure that each person in a group has the means to communicate, understands the importance and the procedure of sending and receiving status reports, and is in fact communicating with the others. Be explicit and clear, in other words, about how and when information will be exchanged within work groups. Make sure that each group is likewise linked.

You will need to consider everything from simple questions, such as where the equipment will be housed and who will be responsible for maintaining it, to more complicated concerns. Do we have someone on staff with enough experience to act as the project manager, or will we have to hire someone? Will the project manager also be the GPS/GIS coordinator, the person responsible for quality-checking all data, and for updating the master GIS database with the GPS data? The coordinator may also be involved in redesigning the database, as the project progresses. As the liaison between the GIS group in the office and the field personnel—people working on the same task but under extremely different circumstances—the coordinator must have a working knowledge of both ends.

To train or not to train

That is the question. Training costs money, but so does not training. Use of GPS is easy enough to seem almost miraculous, but that doesn't mean just anybody can do it. Investing in GPS training can eliminate costly errors in data collection, ensure data integrity, raise quality-control standards, and guarantee compliance with any existing state standards for digital data collection. In Texas, for instance, many state agencies have adopted policies that require any user submitting GPS data to the state to have first passed a certified training course. GPS training benefits all users, from the novice to the expert, as the technology is constantly evolving, in the office and in the field. (And if nothing else, it cuts down on time spent phoning technical support later.)

A GPS collector is only one part of a network, and must understand how the rest of the network functions. It works the other way, too: people performing tasks around data collection need field time with the equipment; it will inform—often crucially—what they do in the office. For instance, a data dictionary for use in the field may be set up very differently from a GIS database. The pieces of a GPS/GIS project are not necessarily puzzling, but they do fit together in a particular way. Comprehensive training—a course that includes basic theory, the principles of integration and database design, an overview of equipment functionality and types, field exercises, differential correction techniques, and use of software packages—is the only way of ensuring that every member of your group understands the function of each piece and its fit with the others. It also promotes good communication later on.

Two: Implementation, or how to get the alligators to pack their bags and leave the swamp

Before: The data dictionary

To create a data dictionary, you will need to think of every feature you want to inventory as either a point, line, or area (referred to in GIS as polygons). For instance, trees, poles, and fire hydrants are points; fences, pipelines, and roads are lines; and land parcels or parking lots are areas. GPS positions are simply latitude/longitude coordinates, with no attribute—i.e., descriptive—data. GPS positions plotted as lines or areas are simply positions joined together, in the chronological order you collected them—a "connect-the-dots" puzzle. You will need to think not only of features to be inventoried and how to define them, but also questions about those features that need to be answered when you are in the field. In a GIS, this type of information is referred to as attribute data. For example, you might want to know a tree's species and height. In your data dictionary, the tree is the feature; the attributes, or questions, are species and height; and the answers to those questions are the values, which will be filled in by the user in the field.

A user can anticipate values found in the field and include those values in the data dictionary. Verifying attribute values is another benefit to performing field reconnaissance. For instance, after working in a certain location for a while, you might decide that you will encounter

only certain species of trees during data collection. As a result, you could define species as a menu choice, listing only the possibilities that you will encounter in that area, creating a "pick list" for the user. You can also include text, numbers, dates, and times as attributes in your dictionary.

A well-defined data dictionary with several menu choices available for tree species; a date and time attribute; underbars between feature names; and units of measurement defined for height.

Before: Lock and load

A data dictionary is a flexible file—you can make changes in it as your project progresses and your needs change. But once it's been set up and loaded into a GPS receiver, most units won't let you edit in the field; that has to be done back in the office using the receiver's accompanying software. Some newer midlevel handhelds, however, do allow field updates. This might be handy if a GPS attribute is not set up like it should be—or it can be a source of trouble. For instance, some fields can be specified as "required": a user can't record a feature unless the required field is filled in first. Lacking the information necessary to fill in the required field, the user could simply delete the requirement. Make sure you want your field collectors to have this kind of discretionary power before purchasing this kind of unit.

You have less flexibility with GPS feature names. In fact, the best idea is to make them identical to the field names in your GIS data, so that the two can be merged after data collection is completed. Defining fields in the GPS unit is not the same as setting them up in the GIS database; features and field names will not be automatically standardized.

Make the files only as wide as they need to be. If you have a feature called "valve," define the feature as a five-character name. (This does not apply to comment fields that depend on input from the user in the field—only to feature names and attribute values. Comment fields can be very long, in some cases up to fifty characters.) Definitions should be as "skinny" as possible: your computer has better things to do with its space.

If any of your feature definitions use two or more words, connect them with an underbar. There should be no spaces in any feature names in a data dictionary. For instance, if you define a feature name as "Fire Hydrant," make sure there is an underbar between the two words, as in "Fire_Hydrant,"or leave out the space and the underbar completely, as in "FireHydrant." If you don't include an underbar, and the data is exported as a space-delimited file, then fire and hydrant will become two separate items in the GIS database.

Attribute names, though often the same from feature to feature, nevertheless must be distinguishable. For example, if you collect a point feature such as a "valve," with attributes called "size" and "type," and another feature, "meter," that also has attributes called "size" and "type"—in other words, multiple features with identical attributes—some GPS software will merge all of the point features into one file upon GIS export. The column may either show up twice, or be eliminated altogether. To avoid this potentially disastrous confusion, give the attribute a two-letter prefix corresponding to the feature name. The attributes of meter and valve, for example, would be named MT_Size and VA_Size, and MT_Type and VA_Type.

Attribute fields must be well defined in the data dictionary to avoid confusion (and bad data) in the field.

Pop quiz: say you are using a GPS receiver to log the locations and addresses of homes. You have decided, logically enough, to define house numbers as a numeric field. Suddenly, you come across a duplex, where the addresses are 123A and 123B. Can a numeric field take character entries?

No. Attribute types can be defined in a data dictionary as a menu choice, as text, or as a numeric, date, or time field. Attributes allow you to use the GIS's analytical capabilities to answer questions. If you define all fields as text fields, you won't be able to run a statistical analysis once the data is in the GIS. The GIS will not recognize the field as numeric, because it hasn't been defined that way. However, as in the above example, there are cases where defining all fields as text may be necessary.

Most GPS receivers will automatically record the date and time a position was taken. Some situations, however, might call for date or time to be recorded as attributes, so that this information can be included in the data you export to the GIS database. For instance, if you are recording the health of the trees in a certain area, looking for disease, you might set up an attribute called "Condition," where the choices are "healthy, unhealthy, dormant." Because data collection for trees is likely to be seasonal, it would be useful to add time and date as an attribute, so that you would know at what time of year the data was collected. This way, a user could query the GIS

database for all dormant trees. If the data was collected in summer, then you know you either have a user who input incorrect data, or a dead tree.

Recording a date and time is also helpful when updates prove necessary—or just helpful. Electrical poles and trees can be damaged by bad weather; new growth in an area may call for an overhaul of the infrastructure. Recording a date and time with GPS data makes it easy to see not only when the data was originally stored, but also each time the feature was revisited—creating, in effect, a history.

The real power of a GPS comes into play in a GIS when locations of specific things (like telephone poles) can be positioned on a digital map with pinpoint accuracy.

Before: Datums and coordinate systems

Imagine your collector entering the height of one tree in meters and another in feet. (Worse mistakes have been made in the field.) The easiest way around this particular pitfall is to select a unit of measurement and include it in the attribute name. This way you can be sure you and your data collector will be singing out of the same songbook.

In the same way, a standard coordinate system will have to be selected. Although there are quite a few of these grids in use today, the most common are Latitude/Longitude, Universal Transverse Mercator (or UTM), and State Plane, which handle horizontal distances, and the geodetic datum, a model of the earth's surface, which includes elevations as well.

Most GPS units collect data using Latitude/Longitude—specifically, the WGS84 datum—as the default coordinate system. It is important to know that the coordinate system the data was collected in will not be converted until that data is exported into your GIS. Most GPS units allow you to change the coordinate system for display purposes only; the data will still be collected using the default system. If the GPS and GIS data are in different coordinate systems, the data obviously will not overlay.

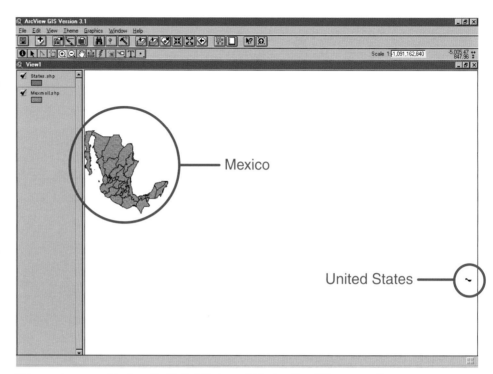

This map is supposed to show the United States and Mexico. Two different coordinate systems were used, however, and as you can see, problems of scale and position prevent the accurate placement of the two countries.

Before: Nuts and bolts, grease and oil

If you've planned properly, now is the time when all the alligators will be packing their bags and leaving the swamp. But before stepping into it yourself, you'll need to set up your equipment.

Create and load a data dictionary into the GPS receiver. (More on this below.)

You decided during the field test how often you were going to collect data; now is the time to configure your receiver for that interval.

Check satellite availability for times of lowest PDOP (positional dilution of precision, also known as GDOP, or geometric DOP), a measure of the angles, or geometry, of the satellites ranged across the sky. The lower the PDOP, the greater the accuracy of the reading. Most midlevel and higher-end GPS units have accompanying software packages that allow a user to forecast satellite positions, and consequently, best PDOP times. Set the elevation mask to screen out satellites that are too low on the horizon to be effective.

You have identified an area for data collection. If the data collection will be done using a laptop or pen computer and PC-MCIA card GPS receiver, then you'll probably want digital maps or aerial photos as background images. If these images are too large to carry on the field computer, then the photos will have to be cropped to match the designated data collection area.

Are the batteries fully charged? Pack spare batteries and cables in case of failure. Check the oil, fill the tank with gas. Give your mom a call.

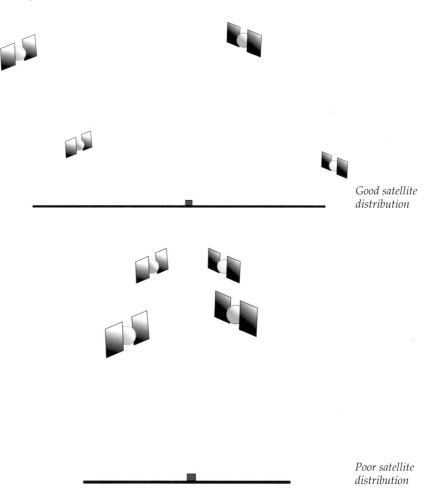

Good satellite distribution

Poor satellite distribution

During: The fun part

The more sophisticated mapping units on the market today have features and functions that can make this part of your project—the collection of data—even easier. For example, the "repeat" function allows you to copy any previously entered attribute information into the next feature. A good time to use this would be if you were, for instance, recording addresses or home locations on the same street. "Repeat" can be used to enter the attribute information from the previous address. Because the street name is the same, and provided that street address is the only attribute information that needs to be entered, you only have to change the house number.

Some GPS units also have a pause button. "Pause" temporarily stops the GPS unit from logging positions. Pausing data logging is a very nice feature to have when you are logging lines and areas and need a moment or two to finish entering attribute information. That way, the GPS unit won't be trying to log a line while you're standing still. "Pause" can also be useful while negotiating hazards and obstructions. The unit will hold while the operator goes around the obstruction and pick up where it left off on the other side. Because GPS positions are joined in time

for line and area features, a straight line will be drawn between the two positions.

Pop quiz 2: You're going about your business, and you meet a landowner who won't allow you on his property. You need to collect a position on that property. What do you do?

Don't panic. You know that your software averages positions to create a point feature. If the landowner's home lies near the middle of his land—and assuming he hasn't let loose his dogs or opened fire on you—you can open the point feature and, using the pause button, take one position at each of the four corners. The unit will average those four positions and *voilà,* there's the house.

Or say you need to map a lake and have access to only one side of the shoreline. Map the shoreline you can get to as a line feature. Then, using a laser rangefinder, map some positions across the lake by using the laser to determine distance. After downloading the collected data, you can create the lake by using the GPS software to trace over the shoreline and the points taken on the other, inaccessible, side.

Because there are so many different methods of capturing data, and because you might have a number of different

people collecting data, it's a good idea to set up some data collection standards—especially if your GPS data may be used in legal decisions. But you want in any case to have airtight, standardized collection procedures that are easy to follow.

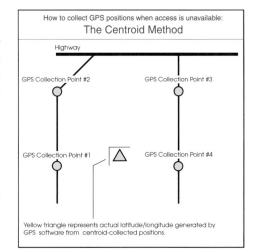

If you cannot physically get to the place where you want to record a position, you can use the pause feature to record positions surrounding it, which will then automatically be averaged.

After: From the field to the kitchen

After the GPS data has been collected in the field, the next step is to download it to a computer in the office, or to a laptop in the field. The tasks that you can do with the software that comes with your receiver will depend on how sophisticated that software is. Although not a GIS, GPS software typically can postprocess, export to multiple GIS formats, and display or print a map. Simple edits can also be done to clean up any data prior to sending it over to the GIS.

The first decision you need to make when downloading your "field-dressed" data is where it's going to be stored. File and data management is essential to any GIS. Will the GPS data ultimately be shared by many different departments?

If so, it might be best to store the data on a server so that everybody can get to it. Who will have write access to the data? In most cases, the GIS coordinator is responsible for clearing all changes, revisions, and updates to the GIS database and resulting layers to ensure data integrity. You will need to consider if the files would best be stored in directories by project, by client, by area collected, or by date.

Once the directory structure has been determined, a cable is used to transfer any collected data from the GPS unit to a PC, through the GPS unit's accompanying software. (Some units transfer data through the PC-MCIA card, eliminating the need for a cable.) The next step is to obtain a base file from an Internet site.

Once a base file has been located, postprocessing can be done by simply following menu choices in the GPS software.

All right, you've collected and corrected your data. The next step is to look at the data using the on-screen map in the GPS software. Some software allows you to pull up a background file and view underlying data as well. Viewing the data on-screen is one way of checking for possible errors. Some software has simple editing tools that allow you to delete GPS positions, or even delete entire features. These editing tools can reduce GIS "cleanup" later on.

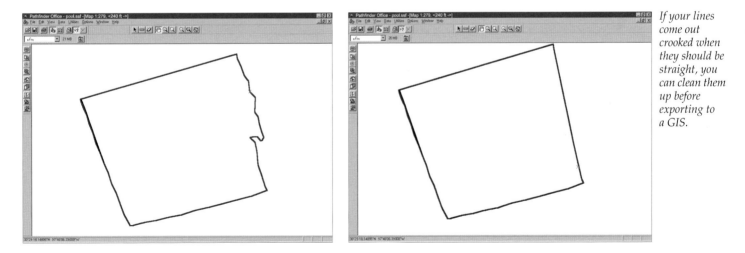

If your lines come out crooked when they should be straight, you can clean them up before exporting to a GIS.

After: From GPS to GIS in one easy step

The next step is to export the GPS data into a GIS format. Most GPS software supports multiple GIS export formats. Once you know what GIS you are going to export to, you will also need to find out what coordinate system and datum the GIS data is in, so that the export data will match. Remember that the GPS data will be in Latitude/Longitude WGS84, the default coordinate system, and won't be changed until you export it to a GIS format and specify another coordinate system and datum.

Once you know what format and coordinate system you need, it's a simple matter to set up the export in the GPS software. Once the export parameters have been set, you press a button. GPS equipment is now in its seventh product generation, and all a user has to do is choose the "shapefile export" option, and *voilà!* a GIS file in ESRI format is at your fingertips. There are several other formats available that are usually acceptable to the various software packages, including DXF (Digital Exchange File), DBF (Database File), and ASCII (text files).

When exporting to a shapefile with some GPS software packages, the latitude/longitude coordinates will not show up as attributes. In ESRI® ArcView® GIS software, you can retrieve the latitude/longitude coordinates simply by moving your cursor over the feature on the map (view). If you want to see the coordinates

in the attribute table, you can export into DBF format and create an event theme in ArcView GIS. When you identify the feature in ArcView GIS, the coordinates will then display in the Identify box.

As the number of GIS data formats has grown, GPS software has become more sophisticated, making it easy to convert raw field data into GIS-ready layers.

Three: Evaluation, or how am I doing?

Now the shadow of judgment must fall on your project. Ask some basic questions: Are you accomplishing what you set out to do? Is there a way you can be more efficient? You may have to consider changes in processes and methodology. Perhaps the data dictionary will need to be revised, or some responsibility reallocated.

A key indicator of success is whether or not a collector had to return to the field. If so, you are probably looking at the tip of an iceberg. Logistics delays and site revisits due to errors in location data are costly, and occasionally dangerous, if field conditions have taken a sudden turn for the worse. A return might be imperative, but if your company is running on a tight budget and a tight schedule, you might be out of luck. Curse the lesson and bless the knowledge: it will help you plan your next project.

Pitfalls

Consider the example of a state agency that did not purchase compatible equipment. This particular agency had established procedures for obtaining and using GIS and GPS technology. Any new GIS or GPS purchases were supposed to conform to those guidelines.

One department, however, giddily purchased $150,000 worth of equipment without consulting the guidelines. The new GPS equipment was ordered from a different manufacturer than the one who'd provided the equipment they already had. Needless to say, the new equipment did not fit the organization's procedures, and is sitting in a storage locker.

Another company, working in the oil fields of east Texas, needed to collect feature and attribute data. Attracted by an inexpensive unit that could calculate real-time differential corrections via the U.S. Coast Guard beacon in Salisaw, Oklahoma, they made the purchase, thinking they were saving money—only to find the unit unable to manage the full scope of the feature and attribute collection they bought the unit for in the first place.

A third group of GPS enthusiasts failed to cultivate an ongoing commitment upon completion of the pilot project. Management could not see an obvious return on their investment of over $10,000 in GPS equipment, locked up the equipment, and fired the only operator who'd been trained to use it! The project was shelved, things were done the way they had always been done before, and the productivity curve flattened. Ongoing support means ongoing education. You must be tireless and consistent in your communication of the real values of GPS usage in your organization.

Finally, remember that poorly trained staff will affect efficiency and consequently productivity. One consultant put it this way: "I always try to get the client to train in-house personnel to maintain any new software or systems I install. It is surprising and disappointing how often that aspect breaks down. The commitment of personnel to project continuation is often a project failing. It results in decreased project value for the client because the data are not readily accessible and are not used effectively. Easy-to-use desktop mapping software has gone a long way to improve this situation (and sometimes impart a false sense of capability), but training is still essential."

Planning is the key. If you take the time beforehand, you won't need it later, when it probably won't be available (if you work in the real world). A little research and comparative shopping up front will eliminate almost everything in the way of foreseeable trouble. If you're concerned about the nearly instantaneous obsolescence that seems to plague consumers as computer technologies grow and change, keep this in mind: the foundation of a good GPS unit is the capability to both postprocess data and correct it in real time. Whatever else changes, your unit will remain viable and valuable for many years if it can perform these tasks.

Fifty thousand miles of pipe

Encountering underground pipelines during construction work has become a dangerous problem as our cities overflow their centers and flood the surrounding countryside. These pipelines and related facilities, often laid decades ago in what were then rural, undeveloped areas, now underlie rapidly growing suburbs, exurbs, and other high-speed development projects.

Most states now have laws that require excavators and builders to "call before you dig." These "one-call" services help builders locate all underground facilities, including pipelines, and consequently, to know where and where not to dig. The Department of Transportation also operates an Office of Pipeline Safety, overseeing interstate pipelines, and individual states may further regulate their portions of interstate lines as well as all in-state systems. The need for accuracy in mapping these mazes of lines goes without saying; the information that pipeline companies supply to governmental agencies, excavators, and builders in compliance with these safety and regulatory laws plays a crucial role in the reduction of risk.

Duke Energy Field Services

Duke Energy Field Services (DEFS) is a major natural-gas-gathering company, with over 50,000 miles of pipeline in the central United States. Over four-fifths of the pipeline now in operation has been acquired from other companies in the last five years—the result of the large-scale acquisition, merger, and sale of facilities that characterizes the energy industry today. Many times during these take-overs and changes of hand, information is lost or inadvertently destroyed. Maps and attribute data collected from other companies may be old and out of date, or have so many different scales of reference that it becomes impossible to figure the actual location of a facility. In the wake of these changes, DEFS found itself with an acute shortage of survey notes, testing reports, and properly detailed maps of its new acquisitions. Sometimes the only document it could get was an executive wall map with a few out-of-date scribbles on it. With field intelligence so compromised, it needed a way to rapidly and accurately locate its assets and enter that information into a master database.

John Linehan, project manager for GIS and GPS at DEFS, describes the situation this way: "We had no way of validating whether the hard-copy or digital data we received was accurate. We had to ask ourselves, 'Do we trust the data?' and 'Can we use it for one-call compliance?' In most cases, the answer was 'No.' We researched several options, including the possibility of geocoding survey notes and

digitizing alignment sheets. Unfortunately, those documents were scarce or missing critical portions of the pipelines. The only other way to get locational accuracy was to locate and resurvey the pipeline, which was too cost-prohibitive. Basically it boiled down to a question of economics, and using GPS to map the pipeline was the most cost-effective option we could find."

Methodology

Before any work could be done in the field, the GPS data-collecting teams had to be selected and properly trained. Nearly all of the collectors were recruited from local field offices, where they worked as cathodic engineers or measurement technicians. Generally well-informed and familiar with their areas, the likelihood of collecting teams losing their way while tracking a pipeline into the bush was negligible, while their detailed knowledge of the facilities they'd be checking would eliminate at least some of the potential sources of confusion. It was hoped they would be able to perform their regular duties as well, reading meters, checking the pipes, and so on. All training was done in-house, with the emphasis on in-the-field, hands-on instruction.

DEFS tried several ways of deploying crews. There were benefits and drawbacks to each, and no clear winner arose at the end of the day. The first method was to have the GPS team grab a back-pack unit (they were using Trimble® Pro-XR/S receivers, a good choice for rugged conditions) and a jug of water, and proceed to walk the line. This was the most accurate method, and allowed for the capture of large amounts of data, but was costly in terms of wages and project duration.

The second method called for a truck or a dune buggy and a two-person team, a driver and a collector (DEFS will not send single collectors into the field because of the potential for injury). The driver traveled the right-of-way, stopping for obstacles—fences, cattle, road crossings, ravines—and of course for features—meters, valves, plants, interconnects, right-of-way markers—at which points the collector would hop out and take a reading. This method is obviously faster, but there are a couple drawbacks, too: getting permission from landowners to drive private stretches of the right-of-way, carrying a large ring of keys and heavy-duty bolt cutters, and the cost of wear and tear on a vehicle used off road.

The third method called on the natural hunting skills of the field agents: GPS collectors were equipped with laser range-finders. This is a quick and convenient way to do business, as the laser hooks directly into the GPS receiver, and can simply be aimed at features in the distance that would otherwise have to be driven or walked to.

The question arose as to how complete coverage needed to be. Collecting all the locations for every facility along every mile of pipe would be time consuming and prohibitively expensive. DEFS wondered if its maps could be accurately and safely updated by verifying only selected key locations, such as valves, interconnects, and road crossings. "We found," says John Linehan, "that by using key locations along the pipeline as registration points, an existing digital map could be massaged into an accurate enough map to be used for compliance and other purposes. Although this method has some drawbacks, the speed of acquisition and processing is cut drastically using this method versus redrafting the entire map from incomplete survey notes." Clearly, the more time spent logging locations, the better the map, but confronted with the reality of 50,000 miles of pipe, the labor—and lodging—costs of keeping teams in the field argued persuasively against completeness.

Finally, receivers packed with extensive and flexible data dictionaries that would allow the collection of point features and attribute information in one pass, developed and field-tested by the GIS team at DEFS headquarters in Denver, the GPS teams were ready to hit the right-of-way.

Data processing and map updating

When the collecting teams returned from the field, they downloaded their rover files and e-mailed them to the GIS processing group in Houston. This group had taken a three-day Trimble-certified training class in GPS, as management believed a comprehensive discussion of all the variables—number and lineup of satellites, dispersion, time, number of points collected—would sharpen everyone's understanding of accuracy, its constituent elements, and what contributes to it and detracts from it.

Trimble's Pathfinder Office software was used to validate, postprocess, and edit the GPS points, and then to convert the data to ESRI shapefile format. The shapefile format allowed each individual point record to be associated with additional attribute data related to that point (such as the condition of the pipe found there). The data was then plotted on top of DEFS's existing pipeline maps. Areas that didn't match were sent to an editing shop in Denver, where the old maps were adjusted to accommodate the newly collected information. The finalized shapefiles were then stored in an ESRI Spatial Database Engine™ (SDE®) database and accessed with ArcView GIS.

The intuitive ArcView GIS user interface and editing tools make it the GIS program of choice for the majority of users (although DEFS sometimes employs CADClient from Autodesk® for some big projects). ArcView GIS may also be used in the field to validate collected data and to quickly generate "first draft" maps following a day of GPS collection.

Obstacles

There was some resistance to GPS initially. Management, for instance, could not understand why only 10 to 20 miles of pipeline could be mapped in a day. As a result, before any GPS work could be started, management was briefed on the complexities and limitations of the GIS and GPS. Another problem, one still of concern, was the lack of staff available to make up the field teams. DEFS had purchased four GPS units, but couldn't find staff enough to keep them in use full time. They wanted to continue using field agents as GPS collectors, but this doubling of duties sometimes proved cumbersome. The final limitation is the sheer size of the job. At the time of this writing, DEFS has been able to complete only a small percentage of the project. Alternatives, such as aerial photography and videography, have been suggested, but cost and accuracy continue to argue against these methods. John Linehan comments: "Nothing can replace the information you get by actually visiting a site."

Accuracy versus expense

The cost of editing, storing, and publishing facility data using a GIS can be—no question—very high. And yet, one erroneous point or feature on a map can have unforeseen consequences. DEFS's budget could not accommodate submeter accuracy and the logging of every point and feature—but neither could it afford many mistakes. Luckily, it found that GPS technology was flexible enough for it to find and take "the middle way." Collecting only key features and surface points cut field time substantially, while the accuracy of the GPS measurements was sufficient to bring its existing maps and documents up out of the danger zone.

John Linehan puts it this way: "We are very happy validating our maps with the GPS. The up-front cost of buying the equipment proved worthwhile, as the decision has saved us money in the long run. We have also saved money when we are required to report to state and federal agencies on compliance issues. Other companies have since adopted our method, using GPS, which proves that we made the right decision."

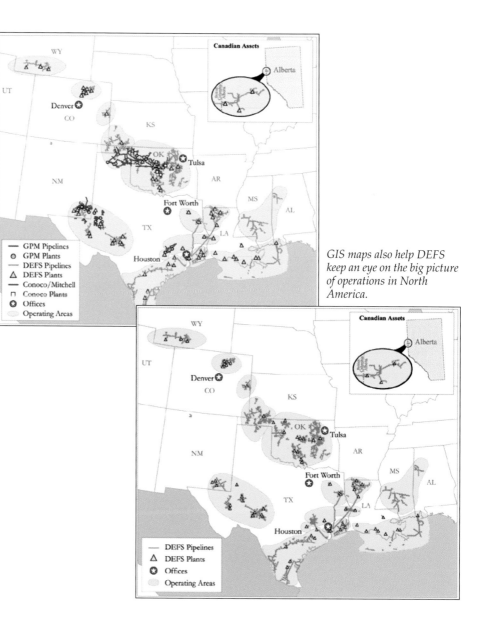

GIS maps also help DEFS keep an eye on the big picture of operations in North America.

Enhanced communication

DEFS realized another unexpected benefit: enhanced communication between
office and field staffs. Because both
groups trained together on GPS, it was
easier for office staff to, for example, call
out to the field for clarification of a collected point, and for the field staff to
understand the request. A GIS technician
may detect imperfections in a data set—
the selected points don't make a smooth
picture—and easily find out if the point is
valid, or erroneous due to some condition or factor in the field, by talking to the
collector. Realities in the field are things
office technicians usually can only guess
at, and an open conduit of information is
crucial; if, as was the case with DEFS,
both ends are equally familiar with software and process, they will communicate
better.

A handy tool to have around

A third benefit of owning GPS equipment
is its ever-broadening range of applicability. Energy companies, for instance, must
routinely locate microwave towers,
meters, and other similar items. GPS was
the natural choice for a basic tool in such
a situation. New uses are popping up
every day, and continuing acquisitions
and mergers make accurate reconnaissance more important than ever. The
faster decisions are made, the more often
minds are changed, and the greater the
chance for errors to creep in and mistakes
to be made. The speed and flexibility of
GPS equipment make it ideal for use in a
fast-paced environment.

Conclusion

Even if DEFS uses the fastest collecting methods possible, it will still take years to adequately capture all the data related to just its current assets. Prioritizing areas and focusing collection efforts on them will make the project more manageable, and advancements in remote technology such as satellite and aerial photography may help cut costs, if properly coordinated with up-and-running GPS/GIS operations. Of course, waiting for technological improvements can work the other way, too, and prove more costly in the end than simply going ahead. John Linehan offers this summary: "The future of GPS data collecting at DEFS is long-term. Right now, we are using in-house collecting teams, but we may turn to contractors to perform this task in the future. The use of a contracting team will reduce time, but the costs are higher and due on delivery. This is something we will have to decide. For now, we are happy with the results of using GIS and GPS and will continue to embrace the technology."

Every company faces these kinds of decisions when new and attractive ways of doing business become available; the newest way is not always the best way. Using the GIS technology with the data gathered by GPS quickly allows a company to obtain, evaluate, validate, and store information pertaining to its pipeline systems. It's clear, for DEFS, that the days of the crumbling, yellowed wall-map, covered with indecipherable hieroglyphics, are over.

Acknowledgments

Thanks to:

John Linehan
Project Manager, GIS and GPS
Duke Energy Field Services
5718 Westheimer
Houston, Texas 77057
www.duke-energy.com

Chapter 5

The reservoir, the vector, and the outbreak

Major epidemics of virulent disease have occurred with surprising frequency throughout human history. Well-known outbreaks—the numerous appearances of bubonic plague in Europe in the late Middle Ages, the pandemic spread of influenza in the United States in 1918–19, HIV-AIDS in our own time—are just the tip of the iceberg. Yellow fever, malaria, and Lyme disease often make front-page news, but less well-known diseases are almost constantly striking one region of the globe or another, moving on and growing in strength, or vanishing as mysteriously as they appeared. As world population growth speeds up, and our cities continue their expansion into previously sparsely populated areas—often rain forests, deserts, and swamps—we face increasing contact with new and strange diseases.

With this increased contact, public awareness, fortunately, is growing, too, and the search for causes and cures is becoming more and more urgent. Consider, for instance, the fact that malaria, a disease we have known how to treat and prevent for years, still causes one to two million deaths per year. Finding the locations of hosts, or "reservoirs," and the means of transmission, or "vectors" (for example, mosquitoes for malaria), are primary tasks as study and tracking of a new disease begins. Once these factors are known, preventive measures can be more quickly and easily applied.

Discovering and understanding the life cycle of a disease calls for painstaking research, literally years of trial and error. For many biologists, it's like solving a gigantic puzzle—which is precisely why the integrated use of the GPS and a GIS can make such a difference.

Photo taken by C. P. McHugh. Used with permission from the University of Incarnate Word.

Humans are most often infected when they live near or are active in the cactus-mesquite habitat favored by wood rats. Here Dr. Kerr uses GPS to record the location of a nest.

Leishmaniasis

Leishmaniasis is a significant health problem in Asia, Africa, India, and Latin America (where varieties, names, and symptoms vary widely), and occurs in tropical and subtropical regions of North America and Europe as well. The World Health Organization describes leishmaniasis as one of the five worst infectious diseases currently active in the world, and estimates that twelve million people, in eighty-eight countries, are infected with the disease, with another 350 million at risk. In its early stages it can easily be misdiagnosed as malaria, and in its later stages resembles leprosy. Leishmaniasis can manifest itself either cutaneously, as spreading lesions and papules, or viscerally, attacking internal organs. Its effects range from the destruction of nasal mucous membranes to fatal damage of the liver and spleen.

Leishmaniasis is caused by a parasitic protozoan, which in turn can infect several hosts and vectors, making it difficult to track and control. The disease also occurs in diverse ecological settings: rural areas, cities, tropical forests, deserts—basically, wherever environmental conditions enable the host/reservoir, vector/transmitter, and parasite to occur together. In the United States, the disease has occurred with the greatest regularity in south Texas.

Dr. Sara Kerr has spent a large part of her professional life studying leishmaniasis. According to Dr. Kerr, associate professor of biology at the University of Incarnate Word in San Antonio, Texas, the first step in the process is to identify potential hot spots, places where the disease may flourish. "South Texas is a good place to start, as the vegetation is right to support rat habitats. We have learned that wood rats are the normal mammalian host, or reservoir, for *Leishmania* in Texas. When we began our study this was simply our hypothesis. However, there are several factors involved, including a sand fly that acts as a vector, which can ultimately transmit the disease from one host to another, including to humans. Basically, the more variables that are involved in a disease, such as transmission by an airborne carrier, the more complex the life cycle is, and the harder it is to track. The habitat that we look at must support both sand flies and rats. Wood rats live primarily in a cactus–mesquite brush habitat, so that is a good starting place."

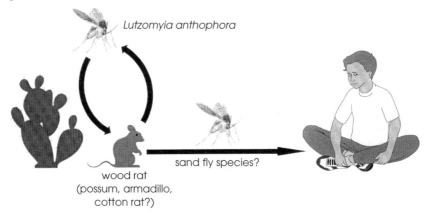

Lutzomyia anthophora

wood rat
(possum, armadillo,
cotton rat?)

sand fly species?

Trapping sand flies and wood rats

Dr. Kerr and her husband, Dr. Chad McHugh, an entomologist at Brooks Air Force Base in San Antonio, work together as a team, and have published several articles detailing their research of leishmaniasis in the United States. They narrowed down the study area (south Texas is a little broad) by looking at areas where human outbreaks had been reported. Dr. McHugh overlaid maps showing the distribution of the southern plains wood rat with the distribution of human cases and saw a distinct correspondence.

Once the reservoir and vector were identified, Dr. Kerr and Dr. McHugh established a long-term study area at an annex to Lackland Air Force Base in San Antonio.

At the research site, rat nests are tagged with numbered stakes. The nests are numbered only if they are active—that is, only if rats are actually found in those nests. To date, ninety-nine sites have been marked.

In the same area, Sherman traps are used to catch rats. Sand fly trapping stations are also set in order to catch and monitor the vector.

GPS is used to record the locations of the traps and the active rat nests. Says Dr. Kerr, "We mark nesting sites, and localities where we have trapped at least one rat, and sand flies. Wood rats are marked with microchips and tested for infection with *Leishmania* on initial capture, then recaptured and retested each season. The abundance and species diversity of sand flies is monitored bimonthly."

"We can also," Dr. Kerr says, "use GPS to map roads or water features that are not found on a map. For instance, our study area has many dirt roads that are not marked on a traditional map."

The group works outdoors in very heavy brush, making a rugged GPS unit necessary. Dr. Kerr chose Trimble's backpack Pro-XR/S unit, which also features a built-in beacon receiver. The study area is close to a U.S. Coast Guard beacon, broadcasting free real-time differential correction data, and making the cost of the extra feature a worthwhile expense.

Once the GPS data is collected, the recorded locations of nests and traps are downloaded from the GPS unit into the GIS database using Pathfinder Office software. The University uses ArcView GIS to overlay GPS data on other maps, and to perform preliminary analysis. It shows the relationship between the trapping sites and the rats themselves, who move around. When the rats are trapped, they are marked with a unique ID. ArcView GIS can then show which rats frequent which nest sites.

"Using GPS and GIS technology together," says Dr. Kerr, "we can detect patterns and traits of both the vector and the host. Although GPS is not used to mark rat trails, these can be drawn in later in ArcView GIS, based on the frequency with which each rat visits each nest."

Loren Rosolowski Witt releases a trapped and tagged rat.

Photo taken by Tommy Hultgren. Used with permission from the University of Incarnate Word.

Magic markers to magic maps

Overall, Dr. Kerr and Dr. McHugh have been happy with the results of their work using an integrated GPS unit and GIS database. Dr. Kerr had been introduced to ArcInfo™ earlier in her career, when working on a project involving the Edwards Aquifer (the primary source of drinking water for the San Antonio metropolitan area), but the program had seemed too complicated for nonspecialists to use. According to Dr. Kerr, "Over time, as ArcInfo and subsequently ArcView GIS became more accessible to the non-GIS specialist, we decided we could use it." Describing the decision to take on GPS technology, she says, "I was frustrated because I am not a good 'mapmaker,' and I wanted a good map illustrating the correlation of sand flies and actual habitats. As the accuracy of GPS technology improved, I knew that I could use it to map habitats, and subsequently determine the spatial distribution of infected rats for *Leishmania* occurrence."

At the start of the project, Dr. McHugh constructed his maps by hand. Host and vector maps were photocopied, and the locations of people infected with the disease were plotted on them with magic markers. The same technique was used to overlay habitat maps. Dr. Kerr talks about using GIS in place of these paper maps: "It's very exciting to me to use GIS, because previously, natural patterns of the earth were hard to visualize. ArcView GIS adds another dimension because we can go beyond our particular

field work and show not only our map of wood rats, but also hundreds of other maps. For example, if we hypothesize that sand flies live near sandy soil or near water, we can support this using other map layers. With the vast amount of data available over the Internet today, we are able to investigate our ecological hypotheses much more easily."

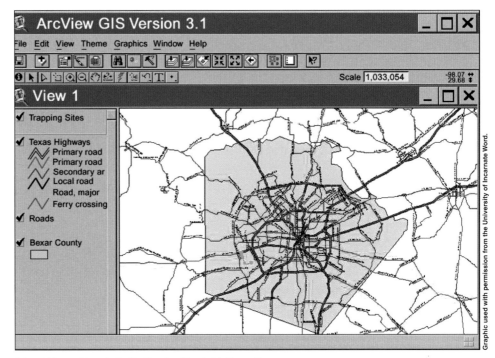

Map of Bexar County indicating Lackland Air Force Base.

We are biologists, not GIS specialists

One of the obstacles faced by Dr. Kerr and her team was the steep learning curve involved with GIS and GPS technology. Dr. Kerr says, "I couldn't do anything until I had training. We are biologists, not GIS specialists. It was absolutely essential to acquire ArcView GIS training. ArcView GIS has so much functionality that trying to use it without any training would've been disastrous. Attending an ESRI–authorized training class substantially decreased the learning curve."

Dr. Kerr also attended a three-day Trimble-certified training class on the use of GPS equipment. Once she felt properly trained herself, Dr. Kerr brought her graduate students up to speed on both equipment and software. The students quickly advanced their knowledge as they began actual field work, combining theory with practice.

Perhaps the greatest obstacle that Dr. Kerr and her team face is one endemic to nonprofit organizations: funding. Currently the group gets its money from the National Institutes of Health, but when that grant expires, the staggering bills for long-term research, hardware, and software will remain—as will the infected sand flies and wood rats.

Markers used to identify active rat nests.

Photo taken by Tommy Hultgren. Used with permission from the University of Incarnate Word.

The density of infected rats

Dr. Kerr's and Dr. McHugh's results have been encouraging. Dr. McHugh was able to isolate *Leishmania* from sand flies associated with an infected wood rat at Brooks Air Force Base. They have also identified occurrences of leishmaniasis in new areas. Using GIS, they identified the reservoir and vector of *Leishmania* in Arizona, where no human cases of leishmaniasis had ever been reported. Upon field investigation, they found infected wood rats 700 miles west of the distribution of human cases.

Because climate and habitat both contribute to the conditions that lead to human infection, there is a weather station at the study area in San Antonio. It records temperature, precipitation, relative humidity, and wind speed, all of which indicate those climatic conditions that are most auspicious for the disease. With the help of the GIS, all of these factors have been overlaid for the first time: climatic factors, habitat, and locations of nests. Seeing how these coincide helps the research team identify places where the disease could spread.

Dr. Kerr elaborates: "The rat-trapping sites were first marked with stakes. By using GPS, these actual locations could be shown as positions on a map. This could not be done previously, as rat nests are in remote areas surrounded by heavy brush. GIS can display the density of infected rats as they are trapped and recaptured. Prior to using GIS, we could not show this information on a map. GPS and GIS make the process, and subsequently the maps, more detailed."

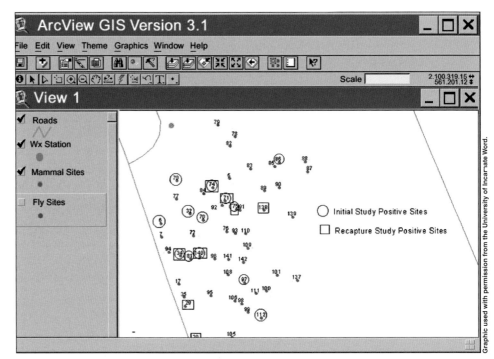

GIS map of numbered trap sites and roads collected using GPS.

Graphic used with permission from the University of Incarnate Word.

Problems of time and space

A chronic problem in this kind of biology is the likelihood of the distributions of the reservoir and vector changing. Flies are also highly seasonal, which makes identifying the factors revolving around them difficult as well. A parasite not limited to movement on the ground, and so radically affected by time, has a small occurrence factor, making windows of opportunity for intensive study few and far between.

The advantage of using GIS technology is that the maps it generates are not only spatial, but temporal. GIS provides for much finer resolution of temporal, seasonal, and spatial prevalence than tools previously available. Dr. Kerr admits that some tasks, such as trapping rats, could be performed without the technology, but agrees that most of the work requires a finer precision. "The distances between rat nests are sometimes only 2 to 3 meters apart. Using a submeter GPS unit, we are able to record the location of each separate nest. The GIS can show a correspondence between abundance of sand flies and infected rats. Previously, we could only say that we had a certain number of rats within a broad infected area. Today, using GIS and GPS, we can produce a map that shows the density of rats' nests within an area of a few meters. The technology provides a much finer level of detail than we could previously achieve."

Dr. McHugh adds that "Technology is not going to replace insights. The GIS can't hypothesize, or realize insights. It still takes a person to perform the analysis." He likes to point out that with or without GIS, the thought process is the same, but that GIS enormously facilitates the process.

Brian Ostrander collects and monitors sand flies.

Photo taken by Tommy Hultgren. Used with permission from the University of Incarnate Word.

Acknowledgments

Thanks to:

Dr. Sara Kerr
Associate Professor
University of Incarnate Word
College of Arts and Sciences
4301 Broadway
San Antonio, Texas 78209

Dr. Chad McHugh, M.P.H., Ph.D.
Entomologist
311th Human Systems Wing
Brooks Air Force Base, Texas 78235

Loren Rosolowski Witt,
Russell Raymond, and
Brian Ostrander
Graduate Students
University of Incarnate Word
College of Arts and Sciences
4301 Broadway
San Antonio, Texas 78209

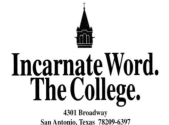

**Incarnate Word.
The College.**

4301 Broadway
San Antonio, Texas 78209-6397

Chapter 6

•••••• "Call 911!"

It's easy to take 911 emergency service for granted. Instead of "Help!" the cry now is "Call 911!" But it wasn't until 1967 that the President's Commission on Law Enforcement and Administration of Justice recommended that a single number be established nationwide for the reporting of emergencies. Before that time (and quite a while after it, too), dialing 0 for an operator was just about the only way to report an emergency. A couple of decades of advances in computer technology made it possible for the 911 system to display phone numbers and addresses of incoming calls, and GIS geocoding—with calls displayed on a map—is now making the system truly workable.

If you live in a city or town.

If you live in a rural area, you probably have a box number on a rural route for an address—data that can't be geocoded in the 911 system.

Because of the problems encountered implementing 911 service in rural areas, the state of Texas passed a bill requiring all rural residents to have street addresses: all roads had to be named, and all houses numbered. This enormous effort had to be organized, coordinated, and implemented statewide. Because a large part of the population in Texas lives in rural areas, it was decided that each county would be responsible for inventorying and addressing their own rural residents. Typically, each county's efforts were directed by a Council of Government, also known as a COG, which functions in an advisory capacity over several counties, cities, and special districts. However, it was up to each county to decide which individual municipal or county entity would be responsible for implementing the 911 addressing.

A modern 911 call-processing center is a fast and effective way of handling emergencies—but only if your road is named and your house is numbered.

Silicon Hills

Austin, the capital of Texas, and its sur-rounding counties are experiencing unprecedented growth. High-tech com-panies and start-ups are flocking to the rolling hills of the region, making it the seventh fastest growing metro area in the United States, and earning it the nick-name "Silicon Hills." Giddings, Texas, the county seat of Lee County, is less than 60 miles east of Austin. Many people have settled in Lee County to take advan-tage of lower tax rates, favorable home prices, and large lots, as well as an easy commute to major Austin employers. With the county's population expected to double in the next five years, Lee County is feeling the effects of population growth, both inside the Giddings city limits and in rural areas.

In 1993, Lee County took on the job of assigning addresses to all residents in rural areas. City and county government entities met to determine the best way to proceed. The Lee County Appraisal Dis-trict had purchased a GIS in 1991, in order to convert hand-drawn maps to a digital format. The district also used the GIS to produce the official county road map and to assign property values to addresses. In light of this experience, it was decided to turn the task of 911 addressing over to it.

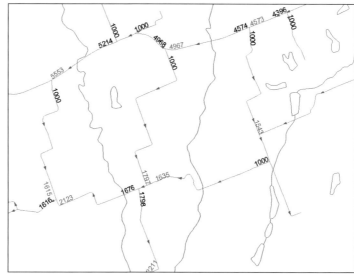

Lee County uses a linear addressing system, while the City of Giddings is addressed on a grid.

A legal pad and another tank of gas

The district began inventorying and assigning addresses in 1994. Because the City of Giddings proper was already addressed on a grid, the district focused on unincorporated rural areas, and decided that—given the lay of the land and the large number of S-curving roads—a linear system, rather than a grid, was the best choice for assigning addresses in these areas.

Roads were divided every quarter mile into street blocks, with each block containing one hundred addresses. Blocks would begin in the 1000 range, so the 1100 block would be a quarter mile down a given road, and the 1400 block would be a mile down the road: an easy way for the drivers of emergency vehicles to know how far down any given road an address might be.

Before they invested in GPS equipment, the Lee County Commissioners' road hands did the job manually. Field workers would put a distance meter in a vehicle and drive county roads. Recording exact footages from driveways to intersections on a legal pad, this information was then manually entered into ArcInfo, which assigned address ranges to every road based on "from-nodes" and "to-nodes." Maps were also printed from ArcInfo and given to county commissioners, who used local knowledge to verify that all roads were on the map.

When the decision was made to get into GPS, the group chose the Trimble PC-MCIA GPS card running on a laptop computer, as that seemed the best solution for a project that included lots of driving. Trimble's ASPEN® software could also display background maps on the PC—again a handy feature to have behind the wheel. Beginning the project with ASPEN's 2–5 meter card, they upgraded to the "gold card," which sharpened the accuracy of their positioning to within a meter.

In the field, GPS was used to assign a physical location, in the form of coordinates, to every address, right on the map. In other words, addresses were assigned based on the GPS location. The GPS unit was also used to drive and record private roads, which are not owned or maintained by the county, and therefore are not part of the original county map database. Lee County is fortunate enough to be within range of a U.S. Coast Guard beacon, so real-time differential correction was available for use at no cost. Once the addresses and roads had been recorded, the real-time corrected information was exported into ESRI shapefile format using Trimble Pathfinder Office software.

Lee County Appraisal District uses a combination of ArcInfo and ArcView GIS software. All of the county's maps are created in ArcInfo, which is also used for geocoding and assigning address ranges to the GPS data. These programs are available to all staff members, who are fully trained in the use of ArcView GIS. Any staff member can locate a specific property or parcel, then build and print a map of it on their desktop. "Basically," says Roy Holcomb, chief appraiser, "any taxpayer can request a map of their property, or an address, and someone in the front office can handle the request, without having to go to the GIS department."

The information is considered part of the public domain, and is shared county-wide. For a nominal fee, the appraisal district provides hard copies of property maps to all taxpayers and anyone living or doing business in the county. Maps and digital data are also provided to the Giddings Police Department, the city, and the county. All county government agencies and departments use ArcView GIS to access the database.

First step

The district had to get up to speed on the GPS unit, and purchased a Trimble-certified training course for the ASPEN unit and software. "I am a firm believer in training," says Roy Holcomb. "It enables my staff to make a faster contribution to our efforts."

Once staff members had been properly trained, the first big question was where to start. The answer was based on the volume of requests the county was receiving for new addresses: wherever the most new residents were arriving would be the area of the county to tackle first.

Second step

The group then developed a simple database containing attributes that could be filled in by the GPS user in the field: name of road, name of city or town, ZIP Code, property owner and identification number, postal address, private road, date, time, and a comment field. The ZIP Code, city, and private-road fields were all menu choices; the rest were "fill in the blanks." Date and time fields were automatically generated and filled in by the GPS unit.

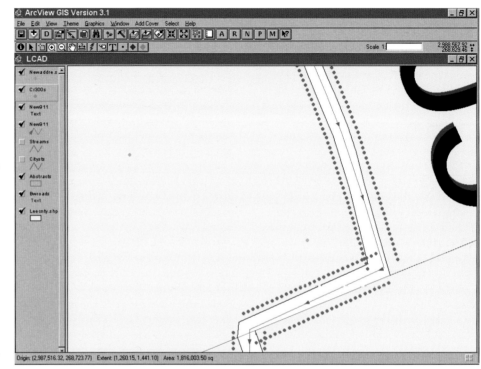

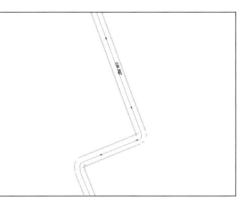

This image shows all of the possible address ranges for county roads in precinct 3. As shown, several addresses can fall on one property. LCAD had to account for future county growth by assigning an address to every possible land parcel, in order to account for situations where land is subdivided after it has been addressed. The GPS is used to determine the exact physical location (within a meter, differentially corrected) of where the address should fall.

Day to day

Appraisers found the "repeat" function especially helpful. Road names did not have to be typed in over and over. They could be typed once and repeated as often as necessary, with only the address numbers changing. Considering the overwhelming number of addresses the appraisers had to record, it's easy to imagine how even the few seconds it takes to type a street name could become an annoyance—not to mention a waste of time.

"Pause," too, was a handy feature, as entrance to or passage through some properties proved difficult to negotiate. Used with the centroid method—taking readings at four corners and letting the unit average those positions—the pause button proved to be an invaluable time-saver.

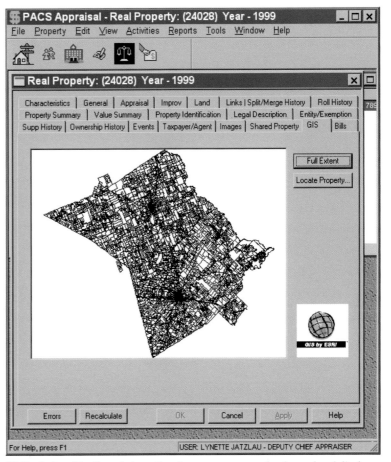

PACs, designed by True Automation, Inc., can query any land parcel and display appraisal maps using an ESRI MapObjects® link to the GIS database.

Developers and oil people

Lee County Appraisal District has been happy with its investment in GPS equipment and the way it has facilitated the enormous job of assigning 911 addresses. The district realized early on, too, that the equipment would be useful for other tasks. Roy Holcomb elaborates: "In the future I see the use of the GPS expanding. For appraisal work, we will be able to physically locate structures by driving up to the house and taking a point. We already have a point coverage that locates every structure larger than 500 feet. We can use the GPS to keep that coverage updated."

The district is also able to use the actual results of its addressing work for other purposes. Roy Holcomb: "Although the 911 work is ongoing, we have been able to use the technology to update our database and assign new addresses as the county population grows. For instance, in the northern part of the county there is a developer selling 10- to 20-acre tracts in a rural subdivision for people who want to experience country living and escape the city. The developers request an address so that homeowners can have electricity hooked up. Having already located all potential addresses with GPS, we can use the GIS to assign a temporary address based on all the ranges for that property. This allows the homeowner to receive not only electricity and other utilities, but also basic access to 911 services."

Another direct result of using the GIS and GPS technology has been a much-improved image within the community for the district. "GIS is one of the best PR tools that we have found," Holcomb says. "The community knows that we have a high-quality mapping system. Many people in the oil and gas business use the public system to find leases. Oil people work all over the state, and can come into a rural setting and have a map printed instantaneously. They can ask for what they want from us and receive it immediately. That makes an impression."

The primary purpose of an appraisal district is to appraise property values for tax purposes, and one interesting fringe benefit of using GPS technology has been the appraisal district's ability to provide much more accurate appraisal values. In 1999, the district implemented a new computer system for appraisals called Property Appraisal and Collections, or PACS. PACS is a Microsoft® Windows®-based SQL™ system, which can search for parcels using any field in the database. In addition, PACS can access the GIS system to display the queried parcel. As a result, the database information is not only better, but more accessible. Less time is spent reviewing appraisals. Taxpayers receive faster service, the revenue stream deepens, costs are offset.

The Lee County Appraisal District is a nonprofit organization, Holcomb points out. "Anything that helps our agency recover costs is viewed as a success."

Kudos for now, hopes for the future

Adoption of GIS and GPS technology has gone over extremely well in Lee County. Many hours of brainstorming were necessary just to come up with a way of managing the sheer size of the project. Nothing like it had been attempted before, and GPS technology was new to everybody concerned. Roy Holcomb nevertheless believes it to be one of the best investments his group has ever made. Not only has it been instrumental in extending 911 emergency service, it has improved the district's image and provided taxpayers with a high-quality, user-friendly mapping system. The district's next goal is to get those maps on the Internet.

Acknowledgments

Thanks to Chief Appraiser Roy Holcomb and his helpful staff.

Lee County Appraisal District
218 Richmond
Giddings, Texas 78942
409-542-9618

Chapter 7

Cold lakes and Hot Springs

Welcome to Hot Springs, a historic resort town nestled in the Ouachita Mountains of south-central Arkansas. Surrounded by Hot Springs National Park, beautiful mountain forests, and long chains of lakes, there are numerous opportunities for recreation in the area, and the town attracts large numbers of tourists each year—as well as new residents. The population at last count was around 33,000, but the new census will report significantly higher figures.

The natural resources of the area support more than just the tourist industry, however: the Ouachita River, which flows through southern Arkansas, is dammed and forms three of the area's biggest lakes. While the lakes are heavily used for boating, fishing, and other recreational purposes, two of them, Lake Hamilton and Lake Catherine, are also sources of hydroelectric power.

The number of boats, docks, and marinas in the Hot Springs region is growing as fast as the population.

Entergy

Entergy Corporation is a major force in the energy industry, providing wholesale energy marketing and trading services, power production, distribution operations, and related diversified services. A global company, Entergy owns, manages, or invests in power plants generating nearly 30,000 megawatts of electricity domestically and internationally, and delivers electricity to about 2.5 million customers in portions of Arkansas, Louisiana, Mississippi, and Texas. Under a license issued by the Federal Energy Regulatory Commission (FERC), Entergy operates Hydroelectric Project 271, which consists of managing lakes Hamilton and Catherine and associated hydroelectric facilities. The company uses both GIS and the Global Positioning System to assist in these management tasks, comply with FERC guidelines, and provide information to agencies that manage other aspects of the lake.

Hot Springs is a magnet for retirees, and most of them want to live on the lakes. One important area of responsibility at Entergy revolves around the management of all private facilities along the shoreline: docks, seawalls, boat ramps, and marinas (collectively called "encroachments"). Entergy generally owns the beds of each lake as well as all the shoreline around the lakes, and all lakefront property owners must obtain a permit to place a dock or other facilities on the lakes. Typically, Entergy receives between fifteen and twenty applications per week to place various types of encroachments on the lakes. Prior to using GPS, each application required a site inspection that included measuring distances between existing docks, across coves, and between other encroachments. This amounted to about two days each week devoted to field inspections, and a two-week turnaround time for granting permits.

This historic bathhouse is a holdover from an earlier era of shoreline facilities.

Building a database in a boat

Bobby Pharr, lakes and property coordinator for Entergy in Hot Springs, realized GIS would be useful for natural resources management as soon as he was introduced to the technology at a local GIS conference. In Mr. Pharr's words, "Entergy's Project 271, lakes Hamilton and Catherine, covers a large and diverse geographic area, consisting of both water and land resources, each with many different features that Entergy is responsible for managing. For these reasons, as well as the specific nature of the management tasks involved, the decision to use GIS and GPS together as a resource management tool was a natural choice."

After further research into GIS technology, Entergy decided to acquire aerial photography from a third-party vendor. Ultimately, these pictures would provide the foundation for a GIS database. The group hired a local engineering firm to survey the area and provide control points for the photos. Using 1:2,400-scale aerial photos, GIS maps were produced of the shoreline, boat docks, and all creeks, roads, and other structures within 500 feet of the shoreline. Existing docks were digitized from the aerial photos and converted into a polygon coverage for use in the field. Little by little, a GIS database was built.

After researching GPS equipment options, Mr. Pharr picked the Trimble Pro-XR/S GPS receiver with ASPEN software running on a laptop. Pharr knew he was going to spend most of his data-collecting days in a boat, and wanted to display his aerial photos as background maps for real-time reference. A PC-based GPS unit was the best mobile computing solution.

In the field, the ASPEN software was used to record a position for each address associated with every dock or other shoreline facility on Entergy's reservoirs. The GPS unit could be used to do the mapping either on the water by boat, or on land in a vehicle. "When we map areas on the lake in the boat," Mr. Pharr says, "we can mark the actual dock as a GPS position because we can get into position right next to the dock. However, the houses associated with each dock are offset from the lake. One reason we chose ASPEN is that it has a 'pick feature' option, which allows us to mark the location of the house in the same GPS file as the docks, using our digital maps and aerial photos as a reference."

Once everything in the field had been recorded, the information was exported into ArcView GIS 2 shapefile format using Pathfinder Office software. Postprocessing was not necessary, as the data had already been corrected in real time, using the U.S. Coast Guard beacon in Salisaw, Oklahoma. Mr. Pharr, staff of one, suddenly found himself with new responsibilities: as a GIS manager, he had to learn new skills to properly and effectively input, view, and evaluate the data he collected. Mr. Pharr obtained ESRI-authorized ArcView GIS and Avenue™ training through the University of Arkansas at Monticello's Forestry Department. Trimble Pathfinder Office and ASPEN training were provided on site at Entergy's facilities by an independent consultant. Once his training was in place, Mr. Pharr was comfortable enough to provide in-house training for other Entergy staff members on an as-needed basis.

From field inspections to a digital dock

According to Bobby Pharr, "As a result of building the GIS database and having all of the map layers in-house, time spent in the field has been reduced from two days per week to only half a day. In turn, this improved public relations, because the permitting turnaround time decreased from two weeks to less than one week. The GIS and GPS equipment actually saved money in the long run by reducing site visits. Before GIS, most permit applications would require a field inspection. Now, applicants call in and I can check on the aerial photo or digital maps for the dock, which gives me a good idea of whether that is something that Entergy can permit. We still have to go out in the field for some that are 'iffy,' but not as often as before."

The original purpose behind the purchase of GPS equipment was to streamline the lake permitting tasks, and to comply with FERC guidelines. It didn't take Entergy long, however, to realize that the equipment would also be useful in other ways. Mr. Pharr saw how his GIS database could be put to good use in other areas of lake management. He elaborates: "Simply having the technology has helped us map many things we weren't able to map before, including utility and road crossings, environmentally sensitive areas, project and ownership boundaries, flood data information, recreation study information, locations of buoys, adjacent ownership and structures, land cover, erosion, and boating

hazards and accidents. We map environmentally sensitive areas and wetlands to comply with federal regulations. Overall, GIS and GPS have both enhanced and expanded the management capabilities of the land and water resources."

Another benefit has been increased public safety on the lakes. Because ASPEN is used in the field during regular patrolling of the waters of lakes Hamilton and Catherine, the GPS can be used to record unauthorized encroachments and boating accident locations. An ArcView GIS shapefile of boat density has been compiled and, used with historical information on boating accidents going back to 1980, gives Entergy a good visual picture of where boating activity has increased on the lake over the past few years. According to Mr. Pharr, "Overall, the GIS has improved safety on the lakes. We do not want to grant permits for marinas or build additional boat ramps in areas where there is already a high density of boats, frequent accidents, or potential hazards such as commercial facilities or bridges that could be contributing to the frequency of boating accidents. We share this information with other agencies who are responsible for boating, safety, and enforcement, including the sheriff and the fish and game department."

Entergy's integrated GPS/GIS technology has also proven its worth during the relicensing process for Project 271. FERC relicensing procedures require Entergy to submit project boundary maps, as well

as recreational study maps. In addition, GIS has improved communications between Entergy and state and federal organizations. Entergy shares all of its data with the government agencies that also have a role in overseeing the lake, thereby establishing a sense of cooperation and synergy between all involved parties.

If only the lakes had been smaller

Entergy experienced no serious obstacles implementing GIS and GPS technology. On the contrary, Bobby Pharr says that "the technology has proven itself, and has done exactly what it was supposed to do. We presented a proposal to management that outlined the cost benefits and cost savings. Overall, management has been very pleased. They see the projected results from the original proposal coming true."

Mr. Pharr will admit, however, that there are some things they might have done differently: "We made some mistakes in the process. Some of the contours around the lake were originally digitized as lines, and we wanted closed polygons. These contours were so large that the GIS software could not convert them from lines to polygons. As a result, we had to have several separate polygons to cover the lake, when we would rather have had one polygon to cover the lake, with one set of attributes. However, overall, the GIS has been an invaluable tool for making lake management decisions. We are very pleased with the strides we have made by using the technology."

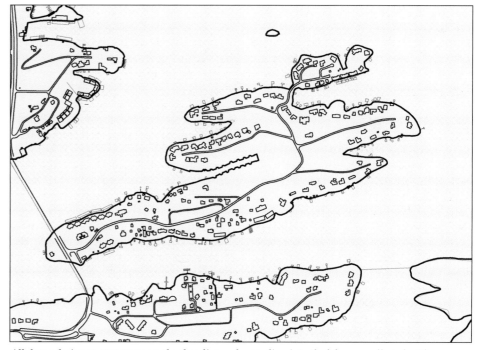

All data relating to structures on the shoreline and extending into the lake was collected with a GPS unit.

Some more ideas

The use of integrated GPS and GIS technology at Entergy continues. As the Hot Springs area grows, GPS will be used to provide updates to the GIS database. Bobby Pharr says that "increased use of the land base will require continuous editing and data inputting which can be done both from the desktop PC and in the field using GPS. We continue to find new uses for the technology. For instance, one county was just readdressed for 911 purposes. However, I definitely don't think I am using the technology to its full extent. I have seen other power companies use ESRI's ArcView 3D Analyst™ to show a three-dimensional representation of their lakes. That would be a great tool to have and put the maps out on our Web site for PR purposes."

GPS is not only making it easier for people to use and enjoy the lakes around Hot Springs—it's making them safer, too.

Acknowledgments

Thanks to:

Bobby Pharr
Lakes and Property Coordinator
Entergy, Hydro Operations
P. O. Box 218
Jones Mill, Arkansas 72105

Chapter 8

Saving the elephants

Imagine yourself on a safari in central Africa: an incredible variety of animals roam the grassy plains. Cape buffalo, giraffes, lions, jackals, the odd rhinoceros, vast thundering herds of wildebeest and zebra—but no elephants. Where, you wonder, are all the elephants? Now, imagine the same trip knowing these majestic creatures were extinct—not only missing but never to be seen again.

Fortunately, there is an organization dedicated to the elephant's survival. Save the Elephants was established in 1993 in response to mounting threats to the elephant's already tenuous hold on existence. Poachers, working a very lucrative ivory trade, have devastated herds across the continent; and as long as that market exists, every elephant is at risk. Habitat loss due to rapidly expanding human populations and increased cultivation of elephant rangeland places added stress on the remaining herds. If their ecosystem is reduced even a little more, the equation is simple: the animals will no longer be able to find food, the population will crash, and the elephant will cease to be.

Save the Elephants is working to secure the future of the elephant population in three basic ways. It assists wildlife departments in the fight against ivory poachers and traders; disseminates information through a variety of local and international media, to boost knowledge of the elephant and its plight; and researches elephant behavior, providing fresh scientific insights into their way of life.

The Save the Elephants mission statement underscores the organization's commitment to the species: "To secure a future for elephants and to sustain the beauty and ecological integrity of the places where they live; to promote man's delight in their intelligence and the diversity of their world; and to develop a tolerant relationship between the two species."

A really big tracking collar

Save the Elephants uses the Global Positioning System to track the movement of elephants, which is the basis of the group's research. Special GPS tracking collars were designed by Lotek Engineering for this project. Iain Douglas–Hamilton, O.B.E., chairman and founder of Save the Elephants, learned of the technology in 1991, and Clair Geddes, Save the Elephants' GIS specialist, has been making maps of elephant movements and aerial surveys for the past seven years. Dr. Douglas–Hamilton says, "We first used GPS to track the flight paths of the aircraft we used in elephant counts, and also record simple waypoint locations of each elephant herd. Our first prototype GPS elephant collar was deployed in 1995. It gave such promising results that I was encouraged to continue development. It was the right technique for the job, as it had the potential for continuous tracking of elephant movements."

Using an internal chip, the GPS collars store data on not only the elephants' positions and activities, but also the outside air temperature. These factors become very important later in the process, when the data is analyzed in the organization's GIS. According to Dr. Douglas–Hamilton, "Our collars can record ambient temperature and motion (by a simple mercury switch). This allows us to relate movement to temperature, an important consideration in elephants, because they have a low surface-to-volume ratio and can easily get overheated when they move. The motion detector allows us to detect periods of sleep or periods of intensive feeding when the elephant does not change position much, but is nevertheless constantly moving its head."

A position is recorded every hour for the first month the collar is on the elephant. Then the GPS is reset to record a position once every three hours. The chip in the GPS unit can store up to 3,640 positions, so even the recording of twenty-four positions a day necessitates downloading only once every five or six months. The downloading software is called GPSHost, also provided by Lotek Engineering. To solve the problem of how to get close enough to the elephants and their collars without disturbing them, downloading sessions are conducted using a laptop computer operated remotely from an airplane flown over the herd.

GPSHost converts the digital GPS data into spreadsheet format. Spreadsheets that are saved in either text (.txt) or database (.dbf) format can then be imported into ArcView GIS software.

ArcView Tracking Analyst

For his research, Dr. Douglas–Hamilton uses a combination of ESRI software and software developed by Dr. Thiemo Krink, of Aarhus University Computer Department. ArcView GIS is used to create maps and take a first look at the data, while the Krink custom program is used for more in-depth analysis. The organization then uses ArcView Tracking Analyst, an ArcView GIS extension, to create maps representing the movements of the elephants. Tracking Analyst can take input from a data source that has x,y coordinates (one form GPS data takes, making it an easy fit), and display that data in ArcView GIS as a shapefile. The benefits of using Tracking Analyst include not only being able to see where the elephants were, but where they were at what particular time. This unique information creates a new path for insight into elephant behavior and can lead to increased knowledge not only of the daily routines of a herd, but of less easily discernible long-term patterns.

Dr. Douglas–Hamilton elaborates: "ESRI software has been invaluable in creating fine detailed maps for lecture or fund-raising presentations. Using these maps, I have been able to raise people's consciousness about elephant issues by showing them what terrain looks like from an elephant's point of view. This clearly demonstrates the effectiveness of protected areas, in particular the national parks, reserves, and private sanctuaries where local landowners or tribal people

have become involved in the conservation process. ArcView GIS and Tracking Analyst are particularly suitable for PowerPoint® computer presentations. I have given dozens of lectures to explain the importance of wise land use in relation to elephants. In particular, Save the Elephants has been able to identify vital corridors that elephants use and to make the case that these areas should be protected for the future."

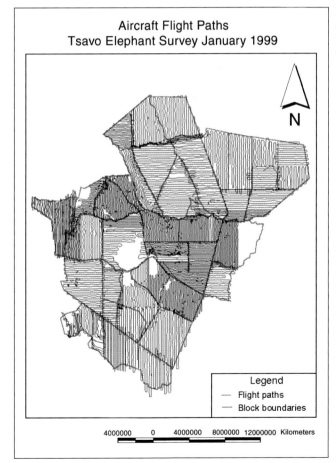

Early on, GPS was used by Save the Elephants to record the flight paths of aircraft during elephant counts.

Day-to-day decisions in the herd

Use of GPS technology by Save the Elephants has provided not only data, but a level of analysis unreachable using conventional research methods. On a broad level, the home ranges of elephants have been described and studied since the late 1960s. However, according to Dr. Douglas–Hamilton, "Before we began using GPS, very little was known about the movements of elephants on a fine scale. Using GPS technology, we have been able to record elephant movements in such fine detail that we can begin to analyze how they make decisions in relation to their needs for food and water, safety from human predators, and the company of other elephants. By understanding their needs we can plan to safeguard their future, for example, by preserving the precise corridors we have defined that they use to travel from one safe area to another."

As a direct result of Save the Elephant's work, more information than ever before is now available about elephants and their behavior. Public awareness and knowledge has also increased. "Elephant movements vary greatly in different areas depending on factors such as safety, food and water availability (itself a function of rainfall), and how many other elephants are around," says Dr. Douglas–Hamilton. "Some elephants have restricted ranges and others roam over huge areas. Save the Elephant's research on the movements of elephants aids in understanding their needs and what

motivates them. This information can then be used to find out how various human and ecological factors influence their movements, and also to reduce conflicts between humans and the elephants."

In one instance, two bulls suspected of raiding crops of a nearby village were collared and tracked. One bull traveled only limited distances, and consequently depended on the crops of neighboring villagers as a food source. The other bull not only traveled greater distances in search of food, but also left the relative safety of Amboseli National Park in

Kenya, foraging in the Longido Controlled Game Area, where he could potentially be killed by hunters or poachers. About the same time, while the study was going on, the Tanzanian National Government made the decision to close elephant hunting in the game area because hunting was an activity incompatible with the objectives of the neighboring Amboseli National Park. Save the Elephant's research provided scientific proof of these cross-border movements, a possibility which had been vigorously denied by the hunting community.

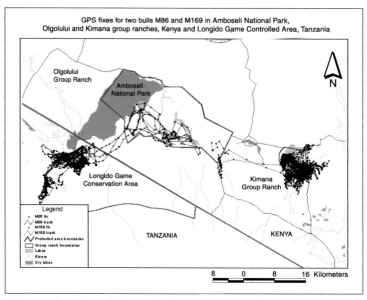

This map shows the individual GPS locations for two bulls, M86 and M169. The GPS positions have been connected by time to indicate each elephant's track. As you can see, one of the bulls wandered out of the protected area of the national park and into the controlled game area.

Recognition, growth, and a better collar

Save the Elephants has seen increased recognition of its work and a concomitant growth of the project itself. Collar design has been refined, and the use of collars in tracking elephants all across Africa has increased tremendously. Since the project began, Save the Elephants has collared more than forty elephants across several regions of Africa. Save the Elephants has also expanded its cooperative work with scientists and conservationists all over the world, providing research support and technical expertise.

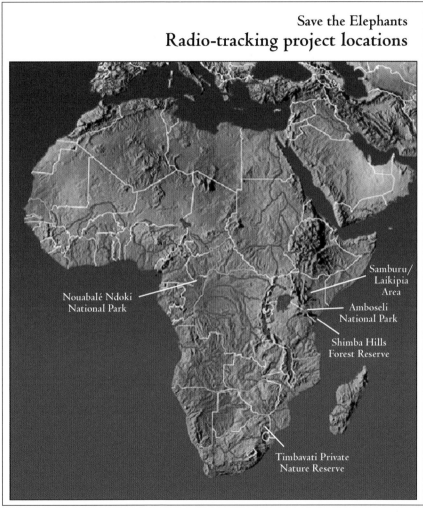

Map depicts Save the Elephants project locations across Africa.

Wind, rain, and several tons of pressure

Elephants present extraordinary challenges to researchers—especially when new technologies are applied to the study. Save the Elephants needed GPS units that could withstand several tons of pressure day after day, as well as exposure to the elements and total immersion in water. Not only can an elephant crush a collar by rolling on it, it can block satellite signals simply by lying down and going to sleep. The GPS collars that Save the Elephants uses are therefore equipped with motion detectors: when motion records fall to zero at the same time GPS positions cease to register, it's safe to assume you've got an elephant on his way to dreamland on your monitor.

Another obstacle was Selective Availability. Working internationally, choices for differential correction were limited. Tracking Analyst does not supply differential corrections, relying instead on the use of precorrected or uncorrected data in the program. For these reasons, Save the Elephants chose to not use any differential correction method. According to Dr. Douglas–Hamilton, "We are not using differential correction at this stage, but would like to do so when we are recording detailed feeding behavior with other observations being made simultaneously with the tracking."

Fortunately, because the range of healthy elephants is so large, a reading off by a hundred meters didn't make much of a difference. Even with S/A on, it was likely that the elephant's location would still fall within the national park or a country's political boundary on a map. With S/A off, the possibilities for fine-tuning tracking information may open new doors of understanding.

An even better collar

Save the Elephants continues to look for ways to improve its research. One of its primary sponsors, Computer Associates, is currently researching a new collar design that will allow the downloading of data in real time directly to the Internet. This will give the organization the ability to display real-time maps showing elephant locations to a much wider audience. Save the Elephants also intends to expand the scope of its studies. One goal is to learn more about the consciousness of elephants, especially as it relates to the ways they talk to each other and, more specifically, the way they deal with death.

In 1998, in collaboration with the Discovery Channel (another primary sponsor), Save the Elephants released an IMAX film titled "Africa's Elephant Kingdom." The film has been praised worldwide and continues to make an important contribution to conservation education, teaching audiences about the diversity of elephant behavior and their way of life. Using a combination of technology and a variety of media formats, Save the Elephants is making great progress toward completing its mission of securing a future on our planet for these great and wonderful creatures we call elephants.

Photo courtesy Jessica Higginbottom, Save the Elephants

An elephant in Amboseli National Park enjoys a light lunch.

Acknowledgments

Thanks to:

Dr. Iain Douglas–Hamilton,
Founder and Chairman
Clair Geddes, GIS Specialist
Save the Elephants
P. O. Box 54667
Nairobi, Kenya
save-eleph@net2000ke.com
www.save-the-elephants.org

Chapter 9

Saving the farmer

We are in the middle of one of the biggest booms in the economic history of our country—but if you try telling that to a farmer who has corn 12 feet high and a profit margin too small to measure, you may get run over by a tractor. Drought, rising operation costs, and falling crop prices are combining in a kind of one-two-three punch that's causing increasing numbers of farmers to overhaul from the ground up the way they do business. They have the same two choices they've always had—growing the same yields at reduced operating costs (for seed, supplies, vehicle maintenance), or increasing yields while holding costs steady—but the means to those ends are changing rapidly.

Advances in the applicability of computer technology—to what has been for most of the last ten thousand years an emphatically nontechnological enterprise—are as much a topic now in farm country as the weather. As farmers become more educated about the ways computers can function on a farm, the more new ideas about reducing costs and increasing yields spring up.

Sometimes there's a gray area between need and solution, between idea and implementation. The other case studies in this book focus on how one particular organization or individual brings together GIS and GPS technology. Agriculture is different: it calls for a special interaction between farmers, or end-users, and lab researchers and consultants, who have the knowledge and experience the farmers need to get the technology—literally—on the ground.

If ever there was an industry that had a crucial spatial component, it is agriculture. GPS and GIS technologies are helping farmers better understand the complex dynamics of working the land.

Precision farming

Basically, GPS and farming come together in this way: Key locations within a field (or within the many different fields that make up a farm) are assigned coordinates with a GPS receiver capable of submeter accuracy. These locations can be places where pesticide levels or types change, where fertilizer levels rise and fall, where soil consistency or conditions change significantly, and so on. Once this field information has been collected, it is downloaded into a GIS, where it can be used to create crop maps that link the newly digitized field data with other kinds of information: slope, pH factors, rainfall records, soil and bedrock geology—again, the possibilities for layers of information are numerous, as are the possibilities for levels and kinds of analysis.

The effect is to put every square foot of a farm at the farmer's fingertips. With pastures, fallow fields, cultivated fields, stands of timber, roads and paths and creeks and ponds all graphically displayed on multiple levels, decision making becomes not only easier but more precise: instead of dropping a uniform number of seeds from row to row, acre after acre, the farmer can pick hot and cold spots and plant accordingly. Likewise, instead of dispensing pesticide at a constant rate, the farmer can spray more heavily where crops have been harder hit, and save both time and money by applying pesticide lightly to less troublesome areas, or not at all.

Getting from coordinate x,y on the computer screen to that same point in the field is also not hard to manage: properly equipped, a tractor can retrace its path and know exactly when and where and how much of a product to dispense. It will all but drive itself.

Precision farming, or information agriculture, has enormous potential power to help pull farming out of its high-cost, low-profit nosedive. The possibility of increased yields—at a time when famine and the threat of famine around the world occur with alarming frequency— is surely welcome news, too. The only problem is the complexity of the technology, that gray area between manufacturer and user.

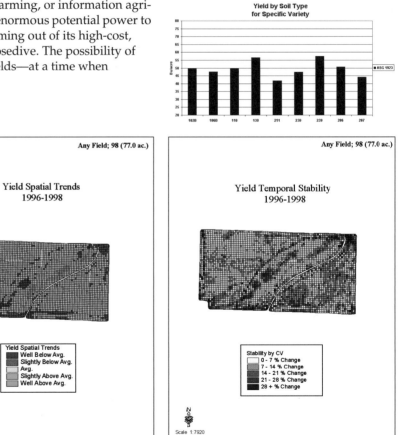

Hitch your wagon to a satellite

This is where a firm like GeoFARM, Inc., enters the picture. A Minnesota company, formed in 1997 in response to a growing demand from farmers seeking new answers to old questions, GeoFARM functions as both a clearinghouse and laboratory. Field and crop information of all kinds—GPS data for instance—is gathered, processed, analyzed, and distributed. GIS technicians turn mountains of data into reports, which are then interpreted by GeoFARM's customers—independent crop consultants, seed company researchers, and agrichemical dealers, who in turn work directly with farmers.

The reports and products generated by GeoFARM include field characteristic map books; nutrient management reports; application maps for fertilizer, lime, and manure; record-keeping reports; yield maps; profit maps; moisture maps; correlation matrices; and statistical comparisons of all documented variables. The software GeoFARM uses to make these reports is powered by an ESRI agricultural applications developer, Site-Specific Technology Development Group, Inc. Maggie Jones, co-owner of GeoFARM (the original SST Information Lab), describes the relationship between the two groups as synergistic. The Site-Specific Technology Development Group provides programming expertise, while GeoFARM and other SST Information Labs manage field implementation and testing. This back-and-forthing ensures that SST Information Lab products actually help farmers and don't cost an arm and a leg.

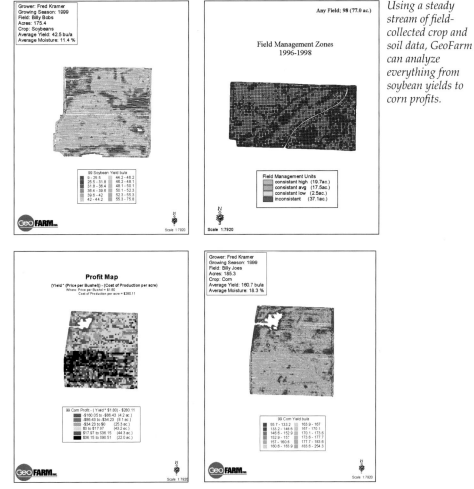

Using a steady stream of field-collected crop and soil data, GeoFarm can analyze everything from soybean yields to corn profits.

How deep is the seed?

Precision farming begins with accurate record keeping. Before planting, it's important to document tillage procedures and the use of preplant fertilizers and herbicides. During planting, the date, seed depth and population, and soil conditions all need to be faithfully recorded. Throughout the growing season, scouting reports need to be filed: what kinds of weeds, insects, and diseases are appearing, what kind of cultivation is going on, what pesticides are being applied, and so on.

Maggie Jones doesn't mince words about this part of the technology: "We emphasize, over and over and over again, the importance of field documentation. This is not glamorous stuff. It's plain old record keeping and it requires discipline and new habits. Therefore it is not popular and is not being quickly adopted. But yield maps, remote sensing, and any other technology that appears glamorous will fall far short of its power without the basic building blocks—field records."

To encourage farmers in this unpleasant task, SST Information Labs offers a simple software program called Field-Book,™ which is customized for each farmer who uses it. Consultants equipped with backpack GPS units (detachable antennas and submeter accuracy make these units the standard) map the farmer's fields, and correct the data via a third-party vendor (or, for those fortunate enough to be in range, a U.S. Coast Guard beacon). This information is then

entered into the FieldBook software, giving the farmer a complete set of boundary maps for every field.

At harvest time, farmers use combines equipped with GPS receivers connected to yield monitors (mass flow sensors that measure grain intake). The same onboard computer the farmer used in the spring to calculate pesticide and fertilizer use now takes in such information as grain weight, location, grain moisture content, time, date, swath width—storing it all on PC-MCIA data cards. The cards are downloaded on a regular basis and this raw

information is sent to the SST lab for processing and analysis.

Using ArcView GIS as the GIS platform, every layer of data is turned into a surface—the seed, the fertilizer, the yield, everything—from which a megasurface is created. "Any record," says Maggie Jones, "machinery performance, crop history, plant population, pesticide application, grain moisture, soil drainage—obtained from a farmer's fields and linked to a location using GPS—is a layer of data that is relevant and useful for analysis."

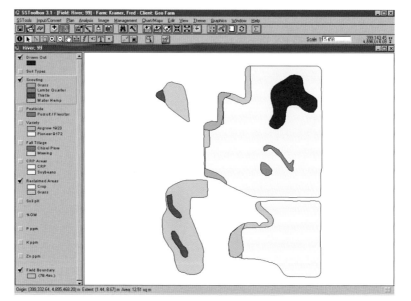

Weed patches and flooded areas documented during field scouting. A field scout wearing a backpack GPS unit marked patches of thistles and other weeds. This map will be used for site-specific, targeted, herbicide application.

Work smarter, not harder

GeoFARM's tools help farmers make decisions that directly affect profitability—even, in some cases, the continuing existence of the farm itself. Questions that used to be simple—like what seed to use—are becoming more and more complex every year. Some hybrids, for instance, are more suited to high pH, and some to low. Others require certain moisture conditions, soil fertility, and so on. In the same field, two hybrids can perform quite differently.

One farmer found he could increase his profit margin by spending less time in the field farming, and more time in his office making management decisions. If that seemed to run counter to common sense, the case made by his field-by-field expense reports and profit maps was persuasive.

Another farmer learned that the yields he was getting from some of his fields did not justify the cost of fertilizer, seed, pesticide, maintenance, and labor that he was putting into them. He set aside the borders of two large fields and placed them, along with several smaller fields, into a conservation buffer strip program. By doing so he not only cut his expenses, he improved environmental conditions in a sensitive watershed. With the money he saved by shutting down those fields that were producing poorly, he was able to invest in other properties with higher yield potentials.

By applying lime at a rate of 2 or 3 tons an acre—but only where it was needed most (a calculation dependent on the pH factor)—a third farmer reduced input costs on a single field of 295 acres by over $2,000. The judicious use of lime also increased his yield in that field, bumping his profit margin even higher.

A less obvious benefit derives from precise record keeping. One farmer was accused by his neighbor of causing a herbicide drift that had damaged crops. The accused pulled out his records for that day, documenting wind direction and the herbicide he'd used—making it pretty clear the complaint was groundless.

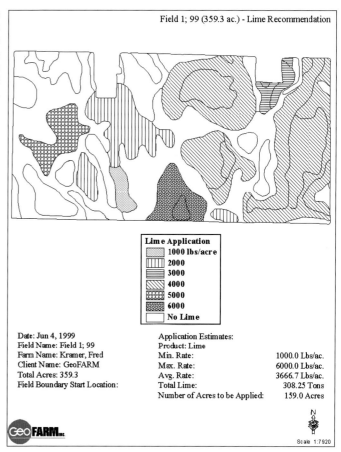

Only 159 acres of this 359-acre field required a lime application. Where applied, rates varied from ½ to 3 tons per acre. This is both economically and environmentally sound.

Field 1; 99 (359.3 ac.) - Lime Recommendation

Lime Application
- 1000 lbs/acre
- 2000
- 3000
- 4000
- 5000
- 6000
- No Lime

Date: Jun 4, 1999
Field Name: Field 1; 99
Farm Name: Kramer, Fred
Client Name: GeoFARM
Total Acres: 359.3
Field Boundary Start Location:

Application Estimates:
Product: Lime
Min. Rate: 1000.0 Lbs/ac.
Max. Rate: 6000.0 Lbs/ac.
Avg. Rate: 3666.7 Lbs/ac.
Total Lime: 308.25 Tons
Number of Acres to be Applied: 159.0 Acres

Scale 1:7920

Fishing in the data pool

One of the greatest advantages of using the services of an SST Information Lab is the opportunity to participate in a pooled database. Data pooling allows agronomic factors to be measured and analyzed on a scale large enough to ensure statistical validity, while giving farmers a chance to consider both the big and the little picture simultaneously, the one feeding into and informing the other. Leaking of trade secrets isn't a problem either: every farmer using GeoFARM services signs a "data privacy and ownership agreement," which allows them to participate or not in the data pool, with their data kept strictly confidential either way.

Maggie Jones puts it this way: "Data pooling is every bit as significant to agriculture as tractors, hybrid seed, or biotechnology. Being able to sort through massive amounts of data is fulfilling our deepest dreams and whetting farmers' appetites for more. The statistical validity possible when using great numbers of sample points and hundreds of replications allows researchers or consultants to rapidly sort through multiple possibilities and narrow them down to a few factors that can then be tested under controlled research conditions. Critical levels for inputs like fertilizers can be fine-tuned. Pest thresholds can be measured. Genetic interactions with environmental and management factors can be studied, and seed genetics can be matched to particular situations."

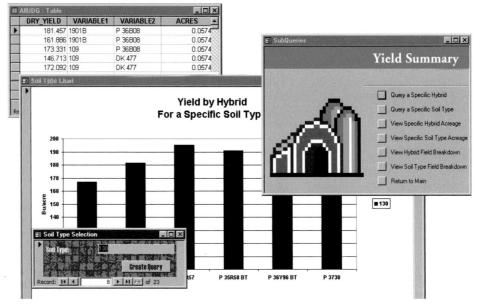

Data collected from participating farms is pooled and processed, allowing individual farmers and consultants to sort swiftly through the pertinent data, perform queries, and get a more accurate "little" picture by looking at the "big" picture.

Rocky roads and rocky fields

Making advanced technologies practical to farmers, making them part of the daily and seasonal routines that have always characterized farming, hasn't been easy. Potential benefits were quickly seen, but the complexities of implementation made for some rough roads as GIS and GPS moved into the agricultural community.

Education and training proved to be the keys to keeping the process in motion. Crop consultants, who already had working relationships with farmers but who did not have the day-to-day responsibilities in the field that farmers had, were in the best position to start the process. Once they'd mastered GIS techniques, they taught the farmers, introducing them to the user-friendly FieldBook, for instance. The various SST Information Labs around the country also held regular training sessions for all comers.

Cost was another factor that couldn't be ignored—neither by the farmer nor by the Information Labs. GeoFARM was formed when two crop-consulting firms realized they couldn't afford to keep up with advances in technology by themselves, and would be better off sharing resources—in much the same way doctors used central facilities for lab work, freeing themselves to see patients.

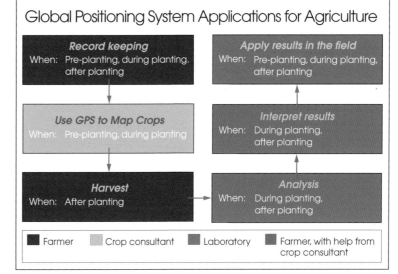

Like any specialized field, digital agriculture analysis has its own terminology, as seen on this attribute screen.

The bridge to the 21st century

Agriculture still means plowing the earth, putting seeds into it, caring for the plants that spring up as a result of that attention, and harvesting what we need to live. The world around that simple process, however, is changing so rapidly and so fundamentally that farmers appear to have little choice about whether or not to adopt new ways of doing business. Farmers work within a tradition that calls first and foremost for independence, for doing things yourself when and where they need doing, doing them right or paying the price. The other half of that tradition, however, has families coming together and lending whatever kind of hand needs to be lent at the first sign a neighbor needs help. It's precisely this combination of qualities—the capacity to work together and remain independent—that will help farmers see GIS, GPS, and other new technologies as ways to build stronger, more profitable, and more enduring farms.

Acknowledgments

Thanks to:

Maggie Jones
GeoFARM, Inc.
50301 230th Lane
Lake Crystal, Minnesota 56055
www.geofarm.com

Dr. David Waits and staff
Site-Specific Technology Development Group, Inc.
824 North Country Club Road
Stillwater, Oklahoma 74075-0918
www.sstdevgroup.com

Chapter 10

Car 54, where are you?

GPS is making this question obsolete. AVL, automatic vehicle location, has rapidly become one of the most heavily used ways of applying GPS technology, especially in business and government. Its most common uses are in managing fleets of commercial vehicles, delivery trucks, and over-the-road eighteen-wheelers, but companies such as OnStar and Lo-Jack are making viable businesses out of tracking personal vehicles. The market showing the sharpest increases, however, is the public safety sector, where the exact location of ambulances, fire trucks, and police cruisers can mean the difference between life and death.

Cops and robbers in the state of Maine

The city of Biddeford, Maine, may be set in one of the most beautiful parts of the country, with a magnificent coastline of sandy beaches, rocky promontories, and the North Atlantic just a few miles east, and rolling hills, pastures, and horse farms reminiscent of Kentucky to the west—and its population (21,000) may suggest crime on a relatively small scale, but that doesn't mean Biddeford's police department doesn't have its hands full.

In March of 1999, unhappy with the time it was taking officers to respond to calls for help, the Biddeford PD decided to install GPS units in its squad cars. It applied for a federal grant, and got enough money to equip nine cars with receivers made by Sierra Wireless specifically for use in vehicles.

A still shot from cruiser-cam footage offers one view of Biddeford officers answering a call.

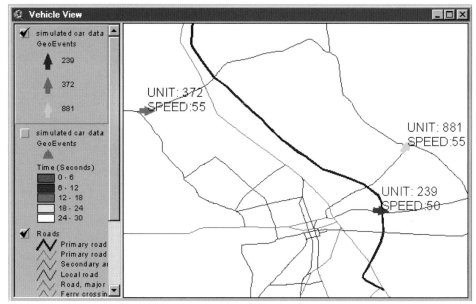

ArcView Tracking Analyst allows police dispatchers to monitor the location and speed of patrol cars in real time.

Black boxes in the trunk, another antenna on top

The receivers, black boxes about the size of two VHS tapes, are mounted in the trunks of the cars, with separate GPS antennas on the roofs. The antennas are a bit out of the ordinary: not only can they receive signals from satellites to determine locations, they can also broadcast those locations as well, to a central monitoring station. Each car is also set up with a computer modem that can transmit the car's GPS coordinates directly to a central computer server, using a local wireless phone service. The advantage to using the modems lies in their capacity to handle real-time correctional data transmitted via wireless or cellular carrier. Real-time corrections can be made over the same modem before sending the GPS data to the server.

Once the signal is transmitted to the server, specially customized software—AVL Listener—translates the raw GPS data and exports it to a shapefile. The shapefile is then sent to workstations housed in each of Biddeford PD's three dispatch stations, where 29-inch monitors display the AVL information. ArcView GIS and ArcView Tracking Analyst, running on the workstations, graphically finish the job.

Tracking Analyst is particularly effective in making the GPS and AVL data not just useful but easy to use. Because it takes input from sources that generate x,y coordinates, the fit with GPS is perfect. Biddeford PD can see not only where its cars are, but where they have been, and when they were there.

The day of the crackly radio signal as the sole link between officers on the street and in the station are gone. Today, dispatchers at Biddeford's command centers track police activity with a variety of digital, voice, and video feeds.

A geography deficit

Sergeant Bruce N. Audie, who's been with the Biddeford PD for twenty-three years, describes the force's predicament before it got into GPS and AVL as one in which it was dealing with "a geography deficit." Response times were too slow, there was confusion sometimes between units as to who was closer to a call, and it wasn't easy to distinguish levels of urgency. Officers closest to the scene of a crime might look up from a nonemergency call they were answering to see another squad car roar past with lights flashing and siren wailing. "Things were done pretty crudely prior to implementing GIS and GPS technology," says Sergeant Audie. "Now, when a call comes in, all the dispatcher has to do is look at the monitor and see who is closest to the incoming call."

The Biddeford PD now trains all its dispatchers to recognize cues that indicate the level of urgency in a call. If, for instance, they hear screaming in the background, their eyes go right to the monitor to see which unit is closest. That unit can be dispatched while the call is taking place.

Using Tracking Analyst's Playback mode, which records and stores GPS locations for later use, has proved quite valuable, too, especially in situations where the department has had to explain or defend its response to calls.

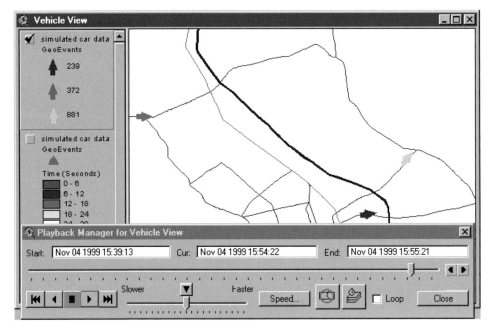

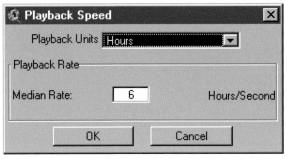

Tracking Analyst can replay events. This feature helps the Biddeford Police Department analyze tactics and decisions made in the field, and also comes in handy as a tool of legal defense.

Novelty to necessity

Biddeford PD dispatchers have come to depend on the ways the new technologies help them do their jobs. "If one monitor goes down," says Sergeant Audie, "we can feel the effects immediately. The dispatchers are all clamoring to get it back. We take for granted what we have in place now. At first, being able to see the police cars on-screen was a novelty, but now it has evolved into a necessity."

Officers, too, have come to appreciate the benefits of the new system. In the early going, there was some apprehension, a feeling that Big Brother was watching. Those feelings very quickly became ones of relief that someone was in fact watching.

The only bump in the road was the realization that they couldn't run ArcView GIS in the squad cars, which had been part of the original plan. ArcView GIS took up too much disk space and memory for the small in-car computers to handle, and using any computer software is problematic in tense situations like high-speed chases, confrontations with weapon-wielding assailants, and other emergencies.

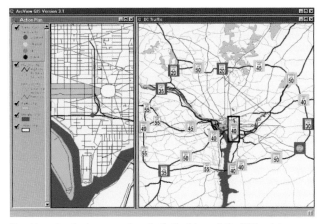

Tracking Analyst can produce both the big and the little picture. This screen shows traffic flow and speed, accident sites, and positions of officers.

Linking 911 and AVL

The system right now stands alone, and is able to display only the locations of police cars. The Biddeford PD would like to be able to link it with Emergency 911 service, and is waiting for the state to finish its compilation of addresses. When that job is done, a 911 caller's address will be displayed on the same monitor showing squad car locations, cutting response time even further.

System designers are also experimenting with dashboard video cameras. Video from these cameras can be uploaded every two minutes on the same wireless network used to transmit the GPS data. There are also plans to use ArcView GIS to interface with crime records, reevaluating statistics by crime class, by neighborhood, by date, and so on. "Basically," concludes Sergeant Audie, "there's no end to what we can use the technology for to help our city and its citizens. It's very satisfying to play a part providing assistance to people in need."

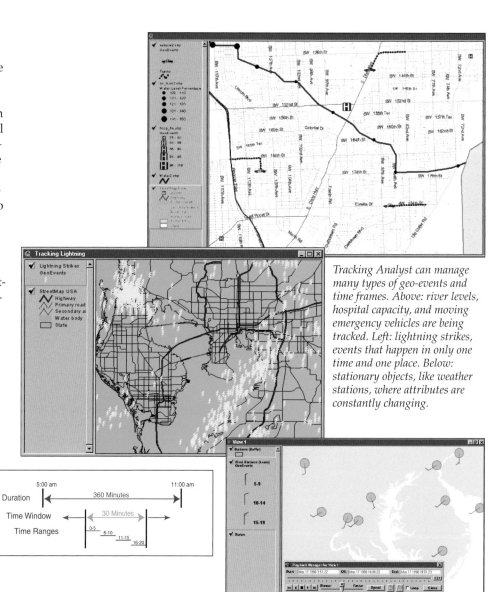

Tracking Analyst can manage many types of geo-events and time frames. Above: river levels, hospital capacity, and moving emergency vehicles are being tracked. Left: lightning strikes, events that happen in only one time and one place. Below: stationary objects, like weather stations, where attributes are constantly changing.

Tracking Analyst allows for the display and analysis of spatial–temporal events in discrete units of time.

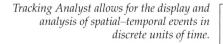

Acknowledgments

Thanks to:

Sergeant Bruce N. Audie and
Chief Roger P. Beaupre
Biddeford Police Department
39 Alfred Street
Biddeford, Maine 04005

Biddeford Police Department Web site:
www.bpd.net

City of Biddeford Web site:
www.biddefordmaine.com

Chapter 11

•••••• Disaster

Flood and wildfire, drought and hurricane, avalanche and earthquake: skyscrapers collapse, entire mountains are burned to a crisp, towns disappear. People die, lose family and friends and homes. The bill for damages rises through the millions of dollars into the billions.

The role pinpoint accuracy of positioning plays in such disasters might seem inconsequential at first glance, but the truth is that GPS and GIS are becoming more and more important—not just in the wake of disaster when, for instance, relief efforts might call for quickly generated maps of flooded areas, for helicopters to navigate through thick smoke, or for the exact location of people buried alive—but in the planning and preparatory phases of emergency management.

Ventura County, California

GPS has been in use at the Ventura County Sheriff's Office since the early 1990s. Because the county is so big—1,872 square miles (almost half of which is the Los Padres National Forest), 42 miles of coastline, and a population of over 750,000—a fleet of helicopters is maintained for search and rescue and wildfire operations. One of them has a real-time navigation system that displays the helicopter's GPS position over street maps or USGS topographic maps.

In 1995, Jim Kniss, manager of mapping services for the Ventura County Fire Department (VCFD), heard about the sheriff's air unit, and thought he saw some great potential benefits of GPS use in dealing with wildfires and other disasters. He decided to test a "proof of concept," and worked with the developer of the moving map system used in the helicopters, AeroComputers, to get GPS data out of their database and import it into ArcView GIS.

The test was a success, and the VCFD quickly began to apply the technology wherever there seemed to be a fit: emergency response, map requests, street centerline maintenance (a vital element in the 911 system), and locations of fire hydrants, water tanks, and obscured or otherwise difficult-to-find buildings.

Jim Kniss gathers data on a fire with a Ventura County Fire Department helicopter in the background preparing for a water drop.

GPS is used by the Ventura County Fire Department on helicopters to map wildfire perimeters. This photo was taken while flying in to record GPS positions to map a fire near Big Sur, California.

Fuel breaks and fire roads

The basic preparedness plan goes like this: GPS units (handheld Trimble GeoExplorer® II models) are used to record the locations of fuel sources and types in high-fuel zones—places where fire is most likely to occur. Fuel breaks and fire roads are also recorded. ArcView GIS is then used to figure times and distances from a potential fire as it spreads. From this analysis a helispot map is produced, showing landing areas within five minutes of each other where water can be gathered.

White water

The Ventura County Fire Department also uses GPS to make "swift-water rescue" maps. The locations of whirlpools that sometimes form near dams, rapids within streams, and other areas of potential danger are recorded. ArcView GIS is then used to identify and map pick-off points, specific water access locations where firefighters can rescue people who have fallen into flood-swollen creeks or riptide-fast flood control channels.

A very popular fire department

News of the VCFD's ability to generate unique and highly useful maps spread fast. The department has since been inundated with requests for every kind of map imaginable. "We produce all the 'hey, can you' maps that we receive requests for," says Jim Kniss. "We have used GPS and ArcView GIS for everything from updating our internal basemaps to producing maps of new fire station locations. We have even mapped hiking trails in the Santa Monica Mountains, to decrease incidences of lost hikers and increase the chances of finding hikers who do get lost."

This photo shows an I-AM-U (Initial Attack Mapping Unit) equipped as a portable workstation for on-scene GIS mapping applications. The I-AM-U is outfitted with counter space, computer, radios, fax-modem, backup power, printers, plotter, and general supplies, all of which are critical during the first twelve to twenty-four hours of an incident. Here, the I-AM-U was recently used during a planning meeting on a controlled burn in Ventura County.

The real thing

When a wildfire does break out, the Ventura County Fire Department works with the California Department of Forestry (CDF). Using the Trimble handheld units, they fly the perimeter of the fire at an altitude of about 500 feet, gathering GPS data every second. Workers on the ground take a position every two to five seconds. The data is then downloaded into a laptop and exported to ArcView GIS. The data is corrected in real time, using a U.S. Coast Guard beacon receiver, or postprocessed using data from RLA Communications, the vendor that sold them their equipment and that also maintains a base station in southern California.

Jim Kniss describes the pre-GPS process this way: "Typically a field observer—the eyes of the incident—ventures into the fire or the flood with a paper map in hand and identifies hazards, buildings, emergency equipment, and most importantly, the perimeter of the incident. This person then returns to the planning unit and transfers the data to a master map showing all of the data that has been collected, which is used to create three to five separate maps." Today, the situation is quite different: "Having GPS and GIS already in place has allowed us to gather perimeter and point feature data quickly and accurately,

which saves valuable time. GPS data can be imported and a planning/tactical map can be produced very quickly. What used to take several hours can now be done in under forty-five minutes, start to finish."

Kniss stresses the danger of over-reliance on GPS data, however. Thick smoke and rough terrain can make even the accuracy of GPS units uncertain. Observations from firefighters in the field continue to be indispensable checks and balances in a system of analysis that requires cool heads and sound decisions in the midst of chaos.

Ventura County Fire Department public information officer Joe Luna uses a map to show the approximate location (using GPS data supplied by the Ventura County Sheriff's Department helicopter) of the Alaska Airlines plane crash off the coast of Oxnard, California.

The California Fire Plan

The California Department of Forestry has a program called the California Fire Plan, developed to encourage landowners and other participants to cultivate their wildlands in such a way that fires entering inhabited areas will encounter newer, more easily contained fuels. For instance, when a fire that has been consuming a thirty- to one-hundred-year-old forest burns its way into a grassland that is less than two years old, it slows down drastically.

Using the ArcView GIS programming language, Avenue, the VCFD has built several ArcView GIS tools and extensions specifically for compliance with the California Fire Plan. Those tools have been a tremendous help to CDF staff as they try to educate and cooperate with farmers and ranchers between Simi Valley and Malibu, a high-fuel corridor that erupts in flames every ten to fifteen years. For these efforts, the VCFD has won numerous awards: the Exemplary Systems Award from the California Geographical Information Association, the Special Achievement in GIS Award, presented by Jack Dangermond at the 1999 ESRI International User Conference, and a citation from the CDF for Outstanding Cooperation and Contributions.

The right stuff?

Pioneers in the use of GIS and GPS in disaster response, one of the biggest hurdles Jim Kniss and his staff had to leap was doubt. There were no guidebooks when they started out, and very few people had even heard of the Global Positioning System. Kniss says they simply had to muddle through and hope everything worked out.

Now the only problem is managing the growth of GIS within the department. ArcView Spatial Analyst and ArcView Network Analyst are propelling movement into new areas. "Right now," says Kniss, "we are producing 2-D drawings, which are basically scanned topo maps overlaid with the fire's perimeter. We would like to start shading slope and aspect on maps. The fuel needs to be at the coldest point of the fire—not where the sun is beating directly down on it."

Virtual fly-throughs are a possibility, too, as is enhanced use of infrared technology that would display heat entities with georeferenced images, and not simply as points on a map. "Our only limit," concludes Kniss, "is simply what we don't think of."

Acknowledgments

Thanks to:

Jim Kniss
Manager, Mapping Services
Ventura County Fire Department
Camarillo, California
805-389-9750
www.ventura.org/fire/vncfire.htm

Chapter 12

Across the ocean single-handed— while millions watch

"La Route du Rhum 98" yacht race

Every four years sailors assemble in Saint Malo, on France's Brittany coast, where they prepare for a grueling race across the Atlantic Ocean, to Pointe-a-Pitre on the Windward Island of La Guadaloupe in the Caribbean. Rounding a single buoy 10 miles east of the starting line, thirty-six boats, 50- to 60-foot mono- and multihulls, and their captains—sailing solo—commence a two- to three-week dash west, toward what was, only a few centuries ago, the edge of the world and an abode of monsters.

The winner in the monohull category in 1998, Thomas Coville, aboard the "Aquataine Innovations," took eighteen days and eight hours to make his run. One dark and stormy night (or at least dark), all alone in the middle of the south Atlantic, his keel became fouled with flotsam. After trying and failing to sail his way backwards out of it, Coville had to dive under his boat and work it free of the debris manually—shredding his hands in the process and almost losing hold of his drifting boat. That he managed not only to stay alive but to win the race on top of it is an extraordinary feat.

But what was almost as remarkable, in a very different way, was the fact that something like two hundred thousand Internet users a day were actively charting Coville's course along with him.

COMMUNICATION

SPONSORING
La Route du Rhum fait le plein

À l'instar de la Formule 1, la course au large est un formidable vecteur de communication pour les entreprises de haute technologie. On pourra effectivement le constater à l'occasion de la 20ᵉ édition de la Route du Rhum, qui reliera du 8 au 21 ou 22 novembre, pour les meilleurs, Saint-Malo et Pointe-à-Pitre. Après Fujifilm, qui, depuis plusieurs années, sponsorise Loïck Peyron et son trimaran *Fujicolor* dans de multiples régates (cette année, le skipper disposera de deux appareils photo numériques MX-700 sur son bateau), c'est au tour de France Télécom et d'Esri de « prendre la mer ». Le pre-mier est partenaire officiel de Thomas Coville, le skipper d'*Aquataine Innovations*. Grâce à cinq caméras disposées sur le bateau (le système de transmission vidéo utilise les satellites Immarsat), le navigateur pourra dévoiler au grand public les réalités de la course au quotidien. L'éditeur de SIG Esri, quant à lui, a été retenu par les organisateurs pour fournir sur Internet la cartographie et le positionnement des compétiteurs. Une occasion unique pour cette entreprise de se faire mieux connaître auprès du grand public en se présentant comme l'un des spécialistes de la cartographie sur le Net.

Using MapObjects Internet Map Server and ArcView Tracking Analyst, ESRI–France established a command center under the auspices of La Maison de la Radio (the French national radio organization), and launched a Web site (http://rhum98.esrifrance.fr) that displayed more than five million user-requested maps online. Working in collaboration with Compaq France, the EUnet, and l'UNCL (Union National des Courses au Large—the managers of the race itself), the team was able to integrate real-time data from the boats—wind, position, speed—with weather reports and other pertinent information (boat specs, pilot bios) in the form of dynamic maps on which race and sailing fans—and Web surfers—could follow the progress of the race. With updates coming regularly every four hours, observers could evaluate each sailor's decisions literally from tack to tack. They could see where the boats were, where they had been, figure how long it had taken them to get from A to B, and calculate how long it might take to get to C.

When Coville was under his boat, in other words, fighting with seaweed and garbage, almost a tenth of the population of France was waiting, on the edges of their seats, eyes glued to terminals, for him to get moving again.

Sailing fans from anywhere in the world could log onto the Web site during the race to track the leaders as they raced their GPS-signal-carrying crafts across the sea.

How the show went on

This brand new form of entertainment came about when ESRI–France formed a partnership with UNCL. Responsibility for the tasks of the project were split down the middle. Race regulations required that all boats be equipped with GPS units linked to an Inmarsat (a system of communications satellites) C beacon (which transmits data bits only). Race managers were in charge of equipping the boats and collecting the data. The pilots needed no instruction in the use of GPS equipment, as transmission was automatic. UNCL would send queries every four hours to each boat via Inmarsat, and the shipboard beacons would answer with positions, speeds, and directions.

ESRI–France, at the radio station command center, received the raw data, entered it into an SDE database, stamped it with the date, recast the coordinates in a Mercator projection, and published the results on the Internet via MapObjects IMS.

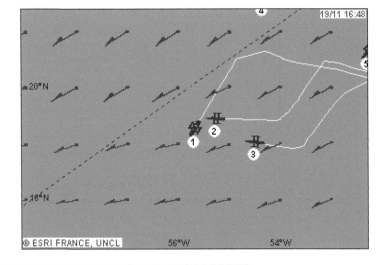

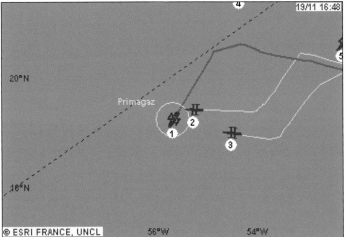

Boat positions weren't the only elements being tracked. Wind speed, direction, and general weather reports were continuously updated.

It worked too well

ESRI–France's Christophe Tourret, who supervised the project, could come up with almost nothing in the way of criticism of the technology. "The only difficulties we had," he says, "were with the IMS—and only because the site was overcrowded!"

Pressed, he will admit to some moments of confusion when the boats passed Cap Finisterre, the extremity of Brittany. "There was an error of datum, between the beacons and our projection routines, rapidly solved when we converted everything to WGS84."

The winners

As the numbers indicate, Internet coverage of La Route du Rhum 98 was immensely popular—not just with the sporting public, but with schoolchildren as well, where educators saw the event as a perfect opportunity to introduce younger students to the basic principles underlying the colorful and exciting maps they were looking at—while at the same time providing some entertainment. The idea that not only does geography matter, but it can be fun, too, was vividly illustrated by this simple unfolding zig-zag of dots across an ocean of computer blue.

The benefit to ESRI was primarily promotional—but not strictly commercial—in nature. Tracking Analyst, as an extension of the basic power of ArcView GIS, represents a significant advance in the way real-time data can be integrated and used in a wider and wider variety of applications. It can be used to display, capture, play back, analyze, and trigger events both spatially and temporally. Data from the boats could be directly fed into the application as it was being generated, where it could be analyzed "on the fly" or "historically."

MapObjects Internet Map Server likewise facilitated race coverage in unique ways. Both vector and raster data could be downloaded and distributed over the Internet, and no time-consuming conversions of databases were necessary, as MapObjects IMS accepts all industry-standard formats.

Bits of data catching the trade winds

What this combination of satellites and software did, in effect, was to put thirty-six "cameras" into play. But instead of transmitting images—in this case, beautiful but ultimately monotonous ones, of waves swelling and breaking to the horizon—these cameras transmitted data, which were in turn transformed into a different kind of image, one in which the relatively slow progress of sailboats across an ocean could be seen as the exciting adventure it actually was.

Acknowledgments

Thanks to:

Christophe Tourret
South regional manager, ESRI–France
ctourret@esrifrance.fr

Jim Baumann
Writer, editor, ESRI
jbaumann@esri.com

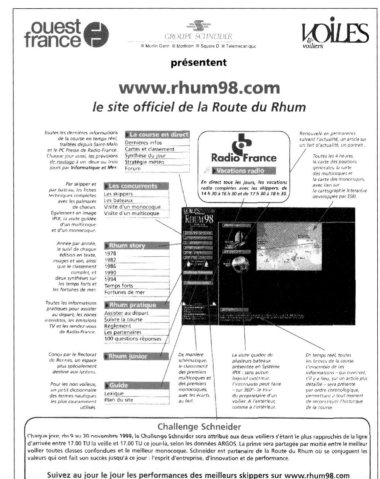

Longitude, Dava Sobel. Walker Publishing Company, Inc. 1995.

911 Telecommunicator's Handbook, Capital Area Planning Council. 1999.

GPS: A Guide to the Next Utility, Trimble Navigation, Ltd. 1993.

Differential GPS Explained, Trimble Navigation, Ltd. 1993.

$14 Billion Worldwide GPS Market by 2005, *GPS World Newsletter,* May 1999.

Could Do Better? *Mapping Awareness,* Trimble Navigation, Ltd. 1995.

Sources of Error. *Mapping Awareness,* Trimble Navigation, Ltd. 1995.

GPS Q&A: Industry Experts Answer Reader's Questions, *EOM,* February, 1998.

GPS Q&A: Industry Experts Answer Reader's Questions, *EOM,* March 1999.

Epidemiology of the Leishmaniases, Alan J. Magill, M.D. *Dermatologic Clinics,* volume 13, number 3, July 1995.

Arthropods: Vectors of Disease Agents, Chad P. McHugh, M.P.H., Ph.D. *Laboratory Medicine,* volume 25, number 6, June 1994.

Tracking African Elephants with a GPS Radio Collar, Iain Douglas–Hamilton, 1998.

http://gauss.gge.unb.ca/manufact.htm
A list of providers of real-time differential correction services.

www. rhum98.com
The official Route du Rhum Web site.

www.save-the-elephants.org
The official Save the Elephants Web site.

www.geofarm.com
The official GeoFarm Web site.

www.sstdevgroup.com
The official Web site of Site-Specific Technology Development Group, Inc.

www.ventura.org/fire/vncfire.htm
The Ventura County Fire Department posts maps, contact information, and prevention tips.

Other books from ESRI Press

ESRI Special Editions

GIS for Everyone
Now everyone can create smart maps for school, work, home, or community action using a personal computer. Includes the ArcExplorer™ geographic data viewer and more than 500 megabytes of geographic data. ISBN 1-879102-49-8

The ESRI Guide to GIS Analysis
An important new book about how to do real analysis with a geographic information system. *The ESRI Guide to GIS Analysis, Volume 1: Geographic Patterns and Relationships* focuses on six of the most common geographic analysis tasks. ISBN 1-879102-06-4

Modeling Our World
With this comprehensive guide and reference to GIS data modeling and to the new geodatabase model introduced with ArcInfo 8, you'll learn how to make the right decisions about modeling data, from database design and data capture to spatial analysis and visual presentation. ISBN 1-879102-62-5

Hydrologic and Hydraulic Modeling Support with Geographic Information Systems
This book presents the invited papers in water resources at the 1999 ESRI International User Conference. Covering practical issues related to hydrologic and hydraulic water quantity modeling support using GIS, the concepts and techniques apply to any hydrologic and hydraulic model requiring spatial data or spatial visualization. ISBN 1-879102-80-3

Beyond Maps: GIS and Decision Making in Local Government
Beyond Maps shows how local governments are making geographic information systems true management tools. Packed with real-life examples, it explores innovative ways to use GIS to improve local government operations. ISBN 1-879102-79-X

ESRI Map Book: Applications of Geographic Information Systems
A full-color collection of some of the finest maps produced using GIS software. Published annually since 1984, this unique book celebrates the mapping achievements of GIS professionals. ISBN 1-879102-60-9

The Case Studies Series

ArcView GIS Means Business
Written for business professionals, this book is a behind-the-scenes look at how some of America's most successful companies have used desktop GIS technology. The book is loaded with full-color illustrations and comes with a trial copy of ArcView GIS software and a GIS tutorial. ISBN 1-879102-51-X

Zeroing In: Geographic Information Systems at Work in the Community
In twelve "tales from the digital map age," this book shows how people use GIS in their daily jobs. An accessible and engaging introduction to GIS for anyone who deals with geographic information. ISBN 1-879102-50-1

Serving Maps on the Internet
Take an insider's look at how today's forward-thinking organizations distribute map-based information via the Internet. Case studies cover a range of applications for ArcView Internet Map Server technology from ESRI. This book should interest anyone who wants to publish geospatial data on the World Wide Web. ISBN 1-879102-52-8

Managing Natural Resources with GIS
Find out how GIS technology helps people design solutions to such pressing challenges as wildfires, urban blight, air and water degradation, species endangerment, disaster mitigation, coastline erosion, and public education. The experiences of public and private organizations provide real-world examples. ISBN 1-879102-53-6

Enterprise GIS for Energy Companies
A volume of case studies showing how electric and gas utilities use geographic information systems to manage their facilities more cost effectively, find new market opportunities, and better serve their customers. ISBN 1-879102-48-X

More ESRI Press titles are listed on the next page ➤

ESRI Press
380 New York Street
Redlands, California 92373-8100
www.esri.com/esripress

ESRI educational products cover topics related to geographic information science, GIS applications, and ESRI technology. You can choose among instructor-led courses, Web-based courses, and self-study workbooks to find education solutions that fit your learning style and pocketbook. Visit www.esri.com/education for more information.

⇐ Other books from ESRI Press ⇐

The Case Studies Series CONTINUED

Transportation GIS
From monitoring rail systems and airplane noise levels, to making bus routes more efficient and improving roads, this book describes how geographic information systems have emerged as the tool of choice for transportation planners. ISBN 1-879102-47-1

GIS for Landscape Architects
From Karen Hanna, noted landscape architect and GIS pioneer, comes *GIS for Landscape Architects.* Through actual examples, you'll learn how landscape architects, land planners, and designers now rely on GIS to create visual frameworks within which spatial data and information are gathered, interpreted, manipulated, and shared. ISBN 1-879102-64-1

GIS for Health Organizations
Health management is a rapidly developing field, where even slight shifts in policy affect the health care we receive. In this book, you'll see how physicians, public health officials, insurance providers, hospitals, epidemiologists, researchers, and HMO executives use GIS to focus resources to meet the needs of those in their care. ISBN 1-879102-65-X

GIS in Public Policy
This book shows how policy makers and others on the front lines of public service are putting GIS to work—to carry out the will of voters and legislators, and to inform and influence their decisions. *GIS in Public Policy* shows vividly the very real benefits of this new digital tool for anyone with an interest in, or influence over, the ways our institutions shape our lives. ISBN 1-879102-66-8

ESRI Software Workbooks

Understanding GIS: The ARC/INFO Method (UNIX/Windows NT version)
A hands-on introduction to geographic information system technology. Designed primarily for beginners, this classic text guides readers through a complete GIS project in ten easy-to-follow lessons. ISBN 1-879102-01-3

Understanding GIS: The ARC/INFO Method (PC version)
ISBN 1-879102-00-5

ARC Macro Language: Developing ARC/INFO Menus and Macros with AML
ARC Macro Language (AML™) software gives you the power to tailor workstation ARC/INFO® software's geoprocessing operations to specific applications. This workbook teaches AML in the context of accomplishing practical workstation ARC/INFO tasks, and presents both basic and advanced techniques. ISBN 1-879102-18-8

Getting to Know ArcView GIS
A colorful, nontechnical introduction to GIS technology and ArcView GIS software, this workbook comes with a working ArcView GIS demonstration copy. Follow the book's scenario-based exercises or work through them using the CD and learn how to do your own ArcView GIS project. ISBN 1-879102-46-3

Extending ArcView GIS
This sequel to the award-winning *Getting to Know ArcView GIS* is written for those who understand basic GIS concepts and are ready to extend the analytical power of the core ArcView GIS software. The book consists of short conceptual overviews followed by detailed exercises framed in the context of real problems. ISBN 1-879102-05-6

ESRI Press
380 New York Street
Redlands, California 92373-8100
www.esri.com/esripress

ESRI Press publishes a growing list of GIS-related books. Ask for these books at your local bookstore or order by calling 1-800-447-9778. You can also shop online at www.esri.com/gisstore. Outside the United States, contact your local ESRI distributor.